COPPERMINE

COPPERMINE

THE FAR NORTH OF GEORGE M. DOUGLAS • BY ENID MALLORY

FOREWORD BY FRANCES DOUGLAS

BROADVIEW PRESS

Canadian Cataloguing in Publication Data

Mallory, Enid L.
    Coppermine: the far north of George M. Douglas

ISBN 0-921149-39-5

1. Douglas, George M. (George Mellis).   2.   Northwest,
Canadian - Description and travel.   3. Travelers -
Northwest, Canadian - Biography.   4. Adventure and
adventurers - Northwest, Canadian - Biography.
I. Title.

FC4167.2.M34   1989   917.19'2042   C89-093691-9
F1096.M34   1989

broadview press
P.O. Box 1243
Peterborough, Canada. K9J 7H5

in the U.S.:
broadview press
421 Center St.
Lewiston, N.Y. 14092

Printed and bound in Canada by
Gagne Ltd.

Contents

for Frances Douglas
who kept the records
and the memories

Acknowledgements

My first debt is to Mrs. Douglas, who gave me not only notes and photos but also her enthusiasm for the North and the part her husband played there.

Dr. George Whalley sent me copies of the Rouviere letters; Elizabeth Whalley and Edna Downes gave me permission to quote from their husbands' books. Professor R.H. Cockburn gave permission to quote from his articles in *Arctic*. Richard Finnie wrote encouragement and reminiscences of his friendship with George and Frances Douglas. Dr. Sylvio LeBlond shared his extensive knowledge of the Douglas family.

Archivists at Trent University, Queen's University and the Public Archives of Canada were consistently helpful. A special thanks to Joy Houston of the National Photography Collection for her cheerful help in finding elusive photos.

My thanks as well to Betsy Struthers, who copy edited the manuscript, and to George Kirkpatrick, who supervised the editorial process and was responsible for layout and design.

Thanks to all the others who helped with information or encouragement. Thanks to Gord Mallory for his long-term interest in this project and for always making my computer behave.

Foreword by Frances Douglas

When, as a mining engineer, my husband, George M. Douglas, agreed to explore the Coppermine River for his cousin, Dr. James Douglas, he read what books could be found describing the area, many written in the eighteenth century by naval men who had reached the Arctic coast by sea. From these sometimes tragic tales he learnt the lesson that every foreseeable contingency, especially conditions of hunger and cold, must be well provided for; that expecting to live off the land was a fallacy. John Hornby who tried to live by that error was rescued more than once by the Indians.

His six prospecting trips spanned those interesting years between the old days when all northern travel was by water or dog team and modern times when a fine bush pilot, though he might not know the name of the lake or river he was flying over, could take you anywhere in a matter of hours.

Before the coming of the planes all trips in the North began on the Athabaska River, whether travelling in one's own canoe or as a passenger on a Hudson's Bay Company steamer, sometimes in a regular convoy of tugs and barges, towing and pushing an incredible volume of freight. The passengers would include Hudson's Bay Company men, civil servants, R.C.M. Police, and personnel for the various Roman Catholic missions. There would also be independent trappers and traders, prospectors and others on some private quest of their own, such as P.G. Downes pursuing his search for the historic Indian still to be discovered beneath the person the white man had made of him.

From this interesting and friendly crowd, half a dozen would carry on a remarkable correspondence with my husband over many years. They move about on the pages of Enid Mallory's *Coppermine* as they did in the North with my husband.

George was not a scientist but understood nature, even when he and nature were at bitter odds. The beauty and determination enchanted him: the dogged trees, the brave bloom, especially the wild roses at Fort Norman which he pressed and sent to me; the wild fruit rushing to brief fulfillment in that rocky land. There was the same rapport with animals, horses, dogs and cats. Once as he approached old Fort Rae, north of Yellowknife, a little black cat ran down to the shore to tell him "all about those dreadful dogs" which in those days ran loose in the summer. At times most of the fish he caught were for wandering dogs.

He was one of those who "could find a world in a grain of sand". I thought of him when I recently came across these 17th century lines from Traherne:

"A stranger here
Strange things doth meet, strange glory see
Strange treasures lodged in this fair world appear."

Frances Douglas

Introduction

The Hudson's Bay Company, early in its trading adventures on the Bay, heard of a river bearing deposits of copper from northern Indians who came to the fort at Churchill River carrying tools made of this metal. It was the lure of rich minerals which led Samuel Hearne, a 24-year-old employee of the Company, to embark on his incredible journeys.

Between 1769 and 1772 Hearne crossed 1500 kilometers of the vast unknown spaces west and north of Hudson's Bay, discovered Great Slave Lake, explored the legendary river to the Arctic Ocean and named it Coppermine.

About 30 miles south-south-east from the river mouth, the Chipewyans showed him their mineral works "... an entire jumble of rocks and gravel." He picked up a small lump of copper. Either the Indians or his own imagination had drawn a much more exciting picture of the copper site, and he was disappointed.

Hearne christened this land "The Barrens." Men of adventure took the name at face-value and shunned it. So through the seasons of another century, the river ran, or mostly lay frozen, almost unvisited by white men. Franklin's party saw it on their 1819-22 journey; his surgeon,

Dr John Richardson, wrote the only description of the copper site to exist until the Douglas party's arrival in 1912.

The pursuit of rich minerals – gold, silver, copper, zinc, pitchblende – has shaped the course of men's affairs throughout recorded time. It has been a strange obsession. Whether the search is motivated by material gain or by the love of the pursuit is unclear. Are the copper and gold an excuse, a rationale which dreamers offer more prosaic men as an explanation for their otherwise inexplicable need to explore, to go where the odds are not good, to overcome formidable obstacles, to suffer and risk death for the sheer joy of moving across the land itself?

George Douglas and the men and women he encountered in the North were all caught up directly or indirectly in the land's enchantment. Few of them actually dreamed of finding copper – some searched for furs, some for souls – but the Coppermine river and Coppermine country exerted a powerful magnetic force on each of them and shaped or altered their lives.

Douglas himself was more explicit than most in his reasons for going North. He wanted to know whether Hearne's Coppermine River did in fact have copper abundant enough to be useful in this new twentieth century. He was a precise man and he knew where he was going. And why.

But even he was not immune to the spell of the Coppermine. After his first trip to the Coppermine in 1911-12, sixteen years passed before he returned to the North and he actually never set foot east of Great Bear Lake again. But his whole life became focused on the barrens and on those he encountered there, both the native peoples and the white explorers, traders and trappers who had become addicted to one of the cruelest environments on the face of the earth.

His beautiful travel book, *Lands Forlorn,* his letters, photographs and diaries, and the articles he wrote for mining journals, provide a sharp record of the end of an era. When Douglas went to the Coppermine in 1911, he was part of the last wave of down-to-earth exploration in the North. When he returned in 1928, there were army planes at Fort McMurray on the Athabasca. Old-time travellers could see the writing on the rocks: the old North was about to disappear.

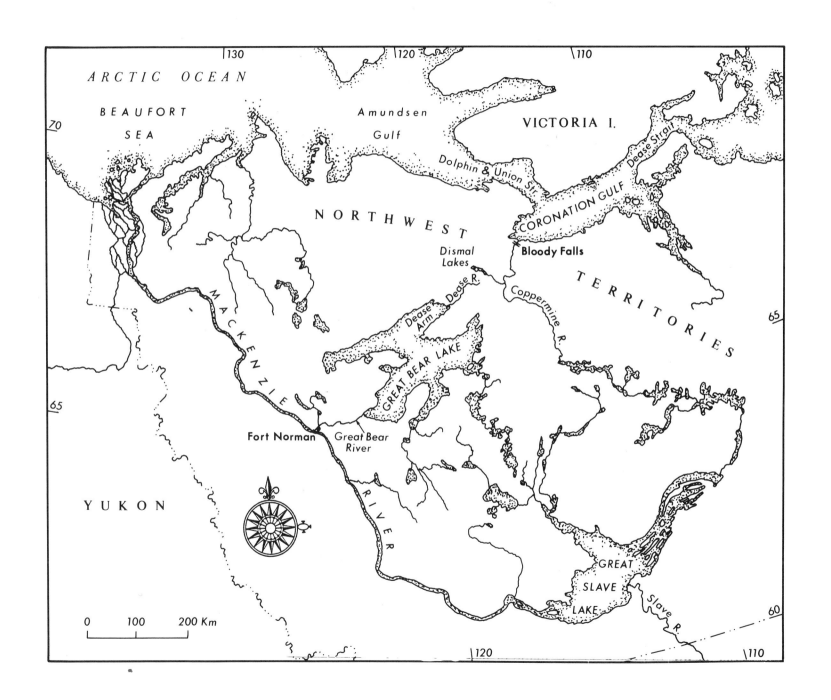

ARCTIC OCEAN

BEAUFORT
SEA

Amundsen
Gulf

VICTORIA I.

70

Dolphin & Union Str.

Dease Strait

CORONATION GULF

NORTHWEST

Dismal
Lakes

Bloody Falls

T E R R I T O R I E S

Dease R.

65

Dease
Arm

Coppermine R.

MACKENZIE

GREAT BEAR LAKE

65

Fort Norman

Great Bear
River

YUKON

RIVER

GREAT
SLAVE
LAKE

Slave R.

60

0   100   200 Km

120

110

Chapter 1
Coppermine Challenge

The last decade of the nineteenth century and the first of the twentieth were an era when gentlemen, Englishmen in particular, were hell-bent on adventure. The whole world had to be seen to be believed. The more difficult the terrain, the more these men wanted to get there.

George Douglas was born in Halifax in 1875 and grew up on a farm near Peterborough, Ontario. His family was not quite typical of Ontario's hard-working, land-clearing pioneer stock: there was a tradition of dragon-slaying in his background. In Scotland his great-grandfather George followed John Wesley when it was dangerous to do so. His grandfather George Douglas was the doctor in charge of Grosse Isle Quarantine Station on the St. Lawrence where in 1847 alone 5000 immigrants died of cholera and typhus. His father, Mellis Douglas, was also a doctor. In 1867 he was awarded the Victoria Cross for saving 17 men at sea on the Indian Ocean off the coast of Little Andaman Island while under attack by natives shooting poison arrows. In April of 1885, during the Riel uprising, Mellis found himself stranded on the South Saskatchewan River with the Canadian Militiamen under Major-General Frederick Middleton, unable to get downstream to the action because their steamer was stuck on a sandbar. Undeterred, he launched a folding canoe of his own design, and paddled 200 miles downriver to set up a hospital at Saskatoon as the casualties came in from the Battle of Fish Creek.

By the time George Douglas was 30, he may have been looking for his own personal dragon to slay. While adventure and tragedy lurked in his background, his own upbringing had been as genteel as life in the backwoods allowed. After Mellis retired from the army, he moved the family from Halifax, first to Quebec City, then to Toronto and then, in 1883, to a farm north of Lakefield, Ontario which he had discovered while attending an American Canoe Association Regatta on nearby Stoney Lake. The new Douglas home, Northcote Farm, was on the shore of Katchiwano Lake just a mile beyond the clearings made famous by Catharine Parr Traill and Susanna Moodie in their writings about pioneer life in Canada.

George Douglas and his brother Lionel did their share of the farm work, paddled canoes to school, helped their father build boats and ran on the logs as the lumber drives moved past their door each spring. The house at Northcote Farm was far from the road so travel was often by water or by ice. Winter evenings were long and isolated. When the boys grew tired of chess, they turned to the books in the Douglas library and read about far-away places.

George's mother died in 1894 and his father, who had run out of money in an attempt to market his folding boats, took the children to England where he rejoined the army. George graduated from Rutherford College and went to sea for three years as engineer with the Allan Lines and the White Star Lines. During idle hours aboard ship, he read voraciously. An aunt had given him a book by the explorer Fridtjof Nansen, called *First Crossing of Greenland* which sparked his interest in the North. One of his mother's uncles, Sir Edward Belcher, had commanded the last naval expedition in search of Sir John Franklin. The adventures of men like Franklin, Belcher and Nansen, and the stories told by big game hunters Warburton Pike and Caspar Whitney about the sub-Arctic region around Great Bear Lake intrigued Douglas.

In 1900 George left the sea and joined the firm of his cousin, James Douglas, in the United States. Born in Quebec, James had worked with T. Sterry Hunt to devise the Hunt & Douglas process for extracting copper from ore. By the turn of the century he had made a fortune in American copper mines with the Phelps-Dodge Company and the Copper Queen Consolidated

Mining Company. He was also president of the American Institute of Mining Engineers. George went to work for him as a combustion engineer in his copper mines in Arizona and Mexico. Mellis Douglas, still in England, had sold Northcote Farm but now that George was on the same continent, he began making trips to Canada, and in 1907 he bought it back. "July 25: A perfect morning, paddled and sailed up to Northcote Farm, saw Jones and talked about the purchase — Northcote Farm is mine."

With this return to Northcote, George established a home base for the rest of his life. But this need to keep some roots intact constituted only half of his personality. He longed for something more demanding than the loveliness of Northcote. Neither the life he led at sea nor the life he now had in Arizona and Mexico satisfied his longing for adventure and exploration.

When cousin James suggested exploring the Coppermine, George jumped at the chance. James explained his younger cousin's enthusiasm this way:

> After years of work in the arid South-west he was naturally seized with an uncontrollable thirst for water, and one day told me of his longing to explore some one of the rivers flowing into the Arctic Sea. Half in jest I undertook to 'grubstake' him, if he would report on the copper-bearing rocks of Hearne's Coppermine River. He accepted the challenge.

So, early in 1911, both George and his brother Lionel returned to Northcote Farm to outfit themselves for a journey to the far North. At 35 years of age, George was a tall fair man with sharp blue eyes and an athletic build. Lionel, two years younger and first officer on the CPR's *Empress of Japan*, had taken a leave of absence to make this trip. They were joined by a third partner, Dr August Sandberg, a Swedish geologist and metallurgist who worked with George in Mexico. None of the three men were married. Their destination was the Coppermine River and the Arctic Sea.

Although he had never travelled much farther north than Lakefield, Douglas was well-versed in the history of the Barrens. By the end of the nineteenth century the North had caught the imagination of the civilized world and inquiring minds gobbled up the published reports of explorers. Douglas read them all.

After Samuel Hearne's odyssey, Arctic exploration focused more on sea than land as the British navy strong and now free from the demands of the Napoleonic wars looked about for something to do with itself. The Franklin expedition of 1820 and 1821 penetrated the Barren Lands and reached the Coppermine. Later Chief Factor Anderson, while searching for the lost Franklin, explored the Great Fish River. This same river was reached by George Back who, in 1833, was looking for another lost party, the John Ross expedition.

But when the searching stopped, the Barren Lands, protected by their austere name and by stories of cruel cold and harsh hunger, lay mostly undisturbed until the 1890s. One exception was a trip financed by the Hudson's Bay Company in 1836. Peter Warren Dease and Thomas Simpson travelled along the Arctic coastline west from the mouth of the Mackenzie, then came back up that river to turn east into Great Bear Lake where they built three small huts which they named Fort Confidence. They nearly froze in those huts as winter came down on the area now known as Dease Bay. In June they crossed to the upper Coppermine and reached the Arctic coast where they turned east. After mapping an amazing length of coastline, they came back up the Coppermine and wintered again on Great Bear Lake.

In 1870 Rupert's Land passed from the jurisdiction of the Hudson's Bay Company to the Dominion of Canada and was named the North-West Territories; then it was left to itself until the century was almost over. The government began to show a little interest in 1895 when it was divided into four administrative districts: Ungava, Yukon, Mackenzie and Franklin.

The Klondike goldrush in 1898 focused new attention on the entire north. In the western Arctic, tales of debauchery, disease and violence to the native people by American whalers, moved the government to establish law and order. In 1903 two men of the North West Mounted Police set up their detachment in a hut on Herschel Island. Meanwhile the voyage of A.P. Low in the *Neptune* for the Geological Survey established the government's presence in the eastern Arctic.

In 1896 the Canadian Geological Survey published the report of J.B. Tyrrell on his epic 1893 and 1894 journeys through the Barren Lands. In 1900 Tyrrell again explored east of Great Slave Lake while two young men, J.M. Bell and Charles Camsell, surveyed along Great Bear Lake and east to the Coppermine.

In the 1890s a new kind of traveller was attracted to the Barren Grounds. These men were not sent by the navy, the government, or the Hudson's Bay Company. They had read the books and were fired with excitement for this last frontier. They plunged into it unafraid of the cold, unaware of their ignorance of native people and geography. Often they were sportsmen seeking big game trophies; sometimes they collected scientific information or specimens. They depended on Indian guides and often became infatuated by the land itself. Usually they published books about their adventures. What these young adventurers had in common was financial independence which allowed them to indulge in exploration and adventure with or without a purpose.

Warburton Pike arrived on Great Slave Lake in 1890, a 28-year-old Englishman who lived on Saturna Island off Canada's west coast. Hunting the legendary musk-ox, he travelled north from Great Slave Lake with Yellowknife guides. Others followed: Frank Russell, an American spurred by scientific interest; Henry Toke Munn, an Englishman who wrote about the spectacle of two million caribou covering the land; and David Hanbury, an Englishman who travelled for 20 months studying the Barren Lands and Arctic coast. Hanbury's account of his travels up the Coppermine and overland to Great Bear Lake were of particular interest to Douglas.

Only two missionaries attempted to enter the Barren Lands. Father Alphonse Gaste travelling with Chipewyan Indians in 1868 reached Dubawnt Lake. Father Emile Petitot, working from Resolution on Great Slave Lake and from Fort Good Hope on the Mackenzie, also made journeys into the Barrens in the 1860s and 1880s

The Royal North West Mounted Police made their first patrol across the Barrens in 1908 when Inspector E.A. Pelletier travelled from Great Slave Lake by the Thelon River to Hudson Bay. Individual traders working for the Hudson's Bay Company or independently made short explorations whenever they could take time from regular work. One of these, James Mackinley, accompanied Pike and later travelled with Hornby and Melville.

The few Barren Land explorers whose work was published were as familiar to Douglas as old friends. Contemporaries like Hornby and Stefansson he had yet to meet. The far-ranging travels of Indians and Inuit across the Barren lands were mainly unknown because their tales were untold in the books he read. Native people did not write down their knowledge of the country. They spoke of important things in their own language and the English or American sportsmen failed to understand. They were mistrusted by the newcomers and in turn mistrusted and sometimes misinformed the adventurers.

Douglas planned his trip with the help of a Geological Survey sketch map (based on the 1900 Bell and Camsell exploration) and David Hanbury's account of his travels. Since Hanbury travelled west, Douglas had to decipher his route in reverse to travel east. His equipment and supplies added up to three-and-a-half tons: food for the whole trip to free them from dependence on hunting and fishing; clothing, bedding, tents; arms and ammunition; two Lakefield canoes and a Peterborough canoe bought in Edmonton; and scientific instruments and camera equipment including tripods, developing tanks and two yards of sateen (very fine woven cotton) with which to cover his Kodak camera when composing and focusing his shots.

Douglas was the first of the Barren Land explorers to extensively photograph the region. With the best equipment James Douglas could supply, he used his camera as a painter would use brushes or a poet would use words to express his reactions to the landscape. In his cabin on Great Bear Lake he developed the pictures with meticulous care and with chemicals carried 4000 miles from home.

He photographed an untouched land so little known in 1911 that names like Hearne and Franklin still stood as beacons and the words of each traveller in this strange land seemed to be engraved on his mind. Their words were not always encouraging.

Father Émile Petitot ventured into the Barrens several times between 1860 and 1880 and found it the most desolate region he had ever visited. Caspar Whitney agreed: in 1896, he called the area between Hudson Bay and Great Bear Lake, "... the most complete and extended desolation on earth." But he also wrote, "To him who has scented the trackless wilds, and whose blood has gone the pace of its perils and freedom, there comes, every now and then, an irresistible impulse..."[1]

Whitney spoke for the adventurers, the men attracted by the euphoria of travel itself. But whether they called themselves sportsmen, scientists or naturalists, none of them were entirely immune to the lure of riches which the very name Coppermine implied. As they plotted their journeys on the blank map of the Barren Lands, they aimed at a river already legendary. A few would reach it, most would not. But it became a focus for their struggle against the elements, a mecca, a mother-lode of excitement and grand challenge, a mysterious place of copper, silver and gold.

To this alluring river moving through its inhospitable land, George Douglas now pointed his finger on a map.

Chapter 2
Athabasca and the MacKenzie

PLATE 1

PLATE 2

PLATE 1

The Douglas party reached Edmonton on May 11, 1911. The Athabasca stage which would carry them the 100 miles north to Athabasca Landing was "... not a single vehicle, but a regular convoy of wagons, and we numbered about twenty-five passengers all told. Our own little party had been joined by Robert Service, who was making a journey to the North with the Hudson Bay Co.'s transport ..."

Service and the Douglas party were perturbed to hear that the HBC brigade of scows by which they were to travel down the Athabasca, had already left the Landing. They hoped that they might still catch them at Grand Rapids, 150 miles down river.

PLATE 2

At Athabasca Landing they spent a frantically busy time dividing their outfit and packing about 1000 pounds into each of two canoes; the rest would follow with a later brigade. The HBC agent insisted on supplying these newcomers with a guide for the dangerous Athabasca rapids.

Douglas described this guide in his book, *Lands Forlorn*: he "... didn't see any fun in paddling. He was worse than useless in camp and no good as a guide ..." When they reached Pelican Rapids, the first dangerous stretch on the river, he "... suddenly got nervous and said it would be necessary to get some one to pilot us down these." No pilot could be found so the Douglas party decided to pilot themselves. The water was swift but its level was high and their canoes came through unscathed.

Even where there were no rapids, this river provided an exhilarating experience, moving them along at a speed of 9 miles an hour so that they covered the 130 miles to Grand Rapids by the third day. Here they caught up with the HBC's brigade.

PLATE 3

"Robert Service knew nothing about canoes or paddling." Shown here in the bow, Service later bought a birch canoe and received some instruction from Douglas.

PLATE 3

PLATE 4

PLATE 4

The Athabasca Brigade of the early 1900s deserves to be famed in story and song. Its purpose was to carry freight 200 miles through the rapids and over the cascades of the upper Athabasca. Its 50-foot scows, glorified packing cases built at the Landing each spring, were broken up for lumber down-river when their job was done.

PLATE 5   PLATE 6

At Grand Rapids the river is divided by an island into two channels about half a mile long. In this distance it drops 40 feet. Here the Douglas party found 25 HBC scows being lightened of their loads. Cargo was landed at the head of the island and carried across in push carts on a primitive wooden tramway. With sweep and pole and skilful dexterity, the Indian and Métis crew took each empty scow down the 40-foot drop and guided it into an eddy at the foot of the island. There, the other men lowered an oar on a line by which the scow was pulled back for reloading. There was always tension, excitement and hard work at Grand Rapids. Sometimes there were accidents, damaged goods and risky rescues.

From the foot of the island, the Brigade began a 90-mile run to Fort McMurray, all of it swift water, with nine or ten formidable rapids. At the Big Cascade a limestone ledge cut across the channel. Here each 10-ton scow balanced like an awkward elephant, half in water, half air-borne, before it took the 5-foot plunge to lower water.

The crew was remarkably adept at this work but occasionally a scow would break its back and the unlucky crew would find itself and its cargo in the water.

PLATE 5

PLATE 6

PLATE 7

The comic-heroic quality of the HBC brigade was not lost on Douglas. "A very slight head wind was sufficient excuse to stop, in fact anything or nothing at all would bring the whole fleet to tie up along the bank for a 'spell.'" The movement or non-movement of the brigade depended entirely on the whims of the Indian pilots. "Our voyage from Grand Rapids to McMurray took a week; this means that we were actually under way about two hours per day; it was a series of resting spells with short interludes of progress. But no one worried, to-morrow was as good as to-day, the weather was fine and bright, the scenery beautiful, and grub plentiful. The Indian crew had four, sometimes five, meals a day; the HBC officers and the passengers had three."

As an added diversion moose or bears appeared occasionally on the banks of the river; "... there were usually at least two or three rifles on each scow and the ensuing fusillade would do credit to a small battle.... The Indian may be a good hunter when he is alone, but when a bunch of them are together any game is fairly secure against damage."

Douglas was condescending and critical of the Indians when he first came north. It took time and experience for him to begin to understand that their ways suited the land where they lived. But in spite of his impatience to get on with the journey, the Indians' enjoyment of life along the Athabasca got through to him. "Our scow journey was altogether thoroughly enjoyable; it was almost a matter of regret when we finally reached Fort McMurray."

PLATE 7

PLATE 8

PLATE 8

Indians receiving treaty payments at Fort McMurray in 1911.

PLATE 9

From McMurray they travelled on the HBC steamer, *Grahame,* to Fort Chipewyan on Lake Athabasca, then down the scenic sand and rock shores of the Rocher and Slave Rivers.

At Smith's Landing on the Slave River, the 16-mile succession of wild rapids running down to Fort Smith ended the voyage of the *Grahame.* Here they despatched all their cargo by wagon along the portage road and walked over themselves.

PLATE 10

This little girl in all her finery on the banks of the Slave River is Catharine Card whose father Gerald is going north with another man to set up a government experimental farm at Fort Simpson.

PLATE 11

The women and children of the Card party wait at the portage under their mosquito hats and surrounded by heaps of cargo.

At Fort Smith passengers could board the HBC's steamer, *MacKenzie River,* but a two-week delay ensued while all the cargo was assembled and loaded. By July 1 they had crossed Great Slave Lake and entered the Mackenzie River, "... a noble river indeed. ... the scenery below Fort Simpson is incomparably grand, a mighty river flowing among mighty mountains."

PLATE 9   PLATE 10

PLATE 11

PLATE 12

PLATE 12

While travelling down the Mackenzie, the Douglas party was able to buy the York boat which they had been eyeing all the way from Fort Smith. She had been towed by the steamer, loaded with the Card party's farm outfit for Fort Simpson. She was a big open boat, 50 feet long, 12 feet wide and 3½ feet deep. They used an old scow tarpaulin to rig her with a sail and named her the *Jupiter*. With good luck and good management they hoped she would carry them across Great Bear Lake.

In the foreground is the Radford and Street expedition. These two young men set out in 1911 to travel by the Thelon River east of Great Slave Lake to Chesterfield Inlet. They then tried to travel with Inuit guides to a whaler wintering west of Point Barrow but they never reached it. This area was so unknown and inaccessible at the time that it was not officially known until 1918 that they had been murdered by their guides.

PLATE 13

The North had a note of warning for the Douglas party before they left the comparative civilization of the river. A hundred miles below Fort Wrigley, where the Salt River flows into the Mackenzie, two trappers had built their shack. Now they both lay dead in their bunks. A passing Indian had discovered them a month earlier. On board the *Mackenzie River* was a Northwest Mounted Police Inspector bound to investigate their shack; he asked the others to accompany him.

One of the trappers had his head blown to a shapeless mass by a soft point bullet from a high power rifle. On a small table beside the other lay a dirty note book and a bottle which still held a bit of carbolic acid. The sight of the men was devastating; the stench was unbearable. It was impossible to remain in the shack for more than a few minutes.

Taking turns, the men managed to break down the bunks and carry the bodies outside. On a scenic slope overlooking the junction of the two rivers, the trappers were buried in a common grave as deep as the men could dig in the frozen ground.

The notebook told the grim tale of what had happened:

> Cruel treatment drove me to kill Peat. Everything is wrong he never paid one sent ship everything out pay George Walker $10. ... I have been sick along time I am not Crasey, but sutnly goded to death he thot i had more money then i had and has been trying to find it.
>
> I tried to get him to go after medison but Cod not he wanted me to die first so good by.
>
> I have just killed the man that was killing me so good by and may god bless you all I am ofle weak bin down since the last of March so thare hant no but Death for me

It was late by the time the trappers were buried. Their furs – the result of a long winter's work – were loaded aboard the steamer. The inquiry held aboard the *Mackenzie River* that night decided that the man shot his partner, then used carbolic acid to take his own life.

PLATE 13

PLATE 14

In the morning the steamer arrived at Fort Norman and the Douglas party and its gear were dumped ashore on the point between the Bear and Mackenzie Rivers. Here was a scattering of log houses and shacks, an HBC store and a Northern Trading Company store, a Roman Catholic Mission run by the Oblate Fathers and a small Anglican Mission church. Bear Rock rose 1332 m (4400 ft.) to the north of the village and the Rocky Mountains loomed to the west. The travellers said farewell to the *Mackenzie River,* to the great Arctic-bound river itself and the help of the Hudson's Bay Company. Now they were on their own.

PLATE 14

Chapter 3
Breakfast at Fort Norman

At Fort Norman, Douglas was introduced to those who would play in the northern drama which dominated the rest of his life. He met Leon Gaudet, the HBC factor, and heard about Joe Hodgson, who had retired from the Company and "who had spent the preceding winter on the Dease River, trapping and hunting caribou."

Jack Hornby, with Cosmo Melville and James Mackinley, a former HBC factor, had just emerged from three years spent on the east end of Great Bear Lake. Hornby's partners were headed south but Hornby seemed to be staying. Douglas met the three men over breakfast on board the Mackenzie River. Melville looked like a man made to conquer the wilds, a big sportsman, over six feet tall, accustomed to giving orders. Mackinley was drunk. Hornby was a tiny blue-eyed man who weighed 100 pounds and stood only five feet, four inches tall. At breakfast he kept dipping his dirty fingers into the sugar bowl to the annoyance of the steamer's captain.

Douglas was surprised to learn that Hornby was the fourth son of Albert Neilson Hornby, a wealthy English landowner and industrialist and one of England's most famous cricket players.

Hornby's oldest brother was also a famous cricket player. His mother, Ada Sara Ingram, was the daughter of Sir Herbert Ingram, publisher and owner of *The Illustrated London News.*

Apparently all this had been a hard act to follow and the young John Hornby went off in several different directions. When he finished his education at Harrow, he trained for the diplomatic corps but never succeeded in passing the examinations. He came to Canada in 1904 looking for something to do with his life. For four years he moved around in the Edmonton-Calgary, cowboy-teamster world. He gravitated to the Yates brothers' 'hobo ranch' north of Edmonton, an establishment of young Englishmen who relished the frontier life of riding, hunting, trapping, freighting goods to Peace River country or doing survey work for the railway. In these years he met Melville, a sportsman who wanted to hunt musk-ox and trade on Great Bear Lake. In 1908 Hornby headed north with him. They were joined by James Mackinley who introduced them to the fur-trading game.

When they first came down the river Hornby and his partners travelled on the *Mackenzie River* with Viljalmur Stefansson and Dr. R.M.Anderson who were heading north to study the Inuit of the Arctic coast. These two went on down the Mackenzie while Melville, Hornby and Mackinley turned east to Great Bear Lake. Before they left Fort Norman, they hired another man, Pete McCallum, a Bear Lake trapper. One of McCallum's assets was an ability to speak the Loucheaux dialect of the Great Bear Indians.

Travelling with a large party of Indians, they made the difficult haul up the Bear River and crossed the great lake to reach its far-east corner. Here they set about building a house on McTavish Bay. In late February an Indian named Michael reported that his party had actually met 'the strangers' and exchanged gifts. The strangers were Inuit. This news caused great excitement among the Indians and the four white men.

In April 1909, the party set out to seek the Coppermine and look for both Inuit and musk-ox. By the time they reached the river some of the Indians were quite jittery. One of them, André, had had a dream which told them not to go on but Jimmy Soldat and Little Bird were very anxious to continue because they wanted the great distinction of meeting "the strangers." The party reached a point from which they could actually see the Arctic Ocean; here the Indians refused to go farther. On the return journey they saw musk-ox and killed six.

In the winter of 1910-11, Hornby moved to a new cabin he built with Melville near the ruins of old Fort Confidence near the mouth of the Dease River. A newcomer, the retired HBC man Joe Hodgson, was there too, in a cabin a few miles away.

That September Vilhjalmur Stefansson made his way overland from the coast and was on the look-out for the Melville-Hornby party. At Big Stick Island, the oasis of trees where Inuit came to make sleds, he came upon Jimmie Soldat still looking for "the strangers." Stefansson, who was travelling with Inuit from the coast, made the introductions and the historic meeting went well. Stefansson then decided to build a cabin for himself and his two companions on the headwaters of the Dease. While the Inuit worked on the cabin, he walked 30 miles to visit Hornby, Melville and Hodgson.

That winter Hornby built a second cabin for a Loucheaux Indian woman named Arimo and her small son Harry. Arimo was a widow although still quite young. She was intelligent, full of humour, and a good travelling companion. Hornby's winter must have been considerably brightened by her presence.

Hornby resented new people coming to Great Bear Lake, but if Douglas was going Hornby longed to go with him. But Douglas, measuring the wiry little man's behaviour and erratic conversation against his great knowledge of the Great Bear-Coppermine country, decided Hornby would not fit in with their party. Douglas's negative opinion of Hornby would not change. Although he would develop a fondness for Hornby and an almost paternal interest in his welfare, he would never consider him an asset.

One other traveller arrived at Fort Norman en route to Great Bear Lake. Jean-Baptiste Rouvière was an Oblate priest from Fort Good Hope; a young man of 30, affable, full of joy and enthusiasm, with a clear purpose shining in his face. He too planned to travel to Great Bear, probably with Hornby. If in the months ahead, Douglas and the others would sometimes question their roles, Rouvière never would. His calling to Christianize the Inuit in that unknown land beyond Great Bear was clear and loud.

From conversations with Hornby, Melville and the priest on the muddy street of Fort Norman, Douglas learned of the events that had set Rouvière on his mission. Each year the Bear Lake Indians made a long hard trip out to Fort Norman for sugar, tea and flour. In December 1910 Hornby sent a letter with them to Father Ducot at the Fort Norman mission, with the news that he had seen the Inuit and offering to help the Roman Catholic church make contact with them.

> [We met] ... eight men, six women and some children. ... The Eskimos and Indians are frightened of each other and it would be dangerous for Indians to try and meet Eskimos without having a white man with them, because the Eskimos have a bad opinion of the Indians. If you intend sending someone to meet the Eskimos, we shall be pleased to give you all the help we can.[1]

Douglas sensed that Rouvière, apart from his high calling, was caught up in the thrill of discovery and adventure. The church was joining a secular push to the last frontiers of Canada. Hornby and Melville had laughed about the sensational publicity Stefansson was getting with his discovery of blue eyes and European features among the "Copper Eskimos." The excitement of the times was apparently not lost on the Church either. To Father Ducot and Bishop Breynat, Hornby's letter was the perfect invitation, an offer of help from a seasoned traveller.

With four years' experience in the North, Rouvière must have had some sense of the magnitude of his task and the harshness of the Arctic world. The Coppermine region was a haunted land made mysterious by its inaccessibility. The breakfast group on the *Mackenzie River* had all read Samuel Hearne's discovery of the copper river and witnessed through his diary the awful massacre at Bloody Falls. They knew about Father Petitot who had wandered into the land beyond Great Bear Lake in 1865 but had been overcome by a fear that the Inuit would kill him. From Warburton Pike, J. Mackintosh Bell and others there were tales of exhaustion, disappearance, near-starvation and always, the deadly cold. Hornby spoke of the undefined shifting no-man's land that existed between Indian and Inuit, into which neither one ventured without fear and trembling.

But Rouvière was not a superstitious man. He had a great faith in the goodness of God and unbounded respect for his superiors who were urging him on. He told the others how Bishop Breynat back in 1904 had written of the possibility of people living north-east of Great Bear. "No-one knows how many they are, or what they are like; but we should like to send a few specimens to Paradise."[2] Rouvière was ready to go ahead and do the nearly impossible cheerfully with the blessing of the Bishop and the help of God.

PLATE 15   PLATE 16

At Fort Norman, Douglas desperately looked for Indians to track his York boat, loaded with three-and-a-half tons of supplies, up the swift Bear River to Bear Lake. He planned to sail across the lake to Dease Bay where he would set up a winter base from which to explore eastward to the Coppermine. But the Indians had no desire to travel with Douglas. "Even the offer of our York boat as soon as we got our stuff across the lake did not tempt them, 'for that' they said 'cannot be divided among us, only one man can own it.'" Moreover, the Indians didn't like the cut of their pants: "... they saw an unfortunate likeness to the uniform canvas pants worn by the RNWMP, and they didn't want any of them in their country."

Douglas, unable to talk to the Indians except through an interpreter, was about to give up his entreaties and travel by canoe, when Leon Gaudet interceded. By offering high wages, he managed to get the Douglas party six Fort Norman Indians, a minimum crew for Bear River tracking.

July 8 was departure day. One of their three canoes was left at Fort Norman in case they had to "get out" a year from now by way of the Porcupine and Yukon Rivers.

The Indian crew arrived at 3 p.m. in a big birch bark canoe which they would use to return to Fort Norman.

> Their names were ... Lixie Trindle, Clement, Samuel, David Wright, Horatio, and François.... François was a small well-built man, very strong, very quiet, and a hard worker so long as he had an example. He had his wife, a little girl, and one dog with him, and he wanted to cross Great Bear Lake, with us, and to work for us a couple of months, which was convenient enough. His wife could talk a little French and was afterward the only medium by which we could communicate with the Indians.

PLATE 16

PLATE 17

Ninety-one miles of the Bear River lay ahead, all of it steeply uphill. For the down-going canoeist, the river was a giant water-slide navigable in a few hours. Coming up, heavily laden with a winter's supplies, the traveller faced a desperate struggle against current and ice; it might take weeks to reach Great Bear Lake.

The first 40 miles were pleasant enough – brilliantly clear water and grass-covered slopes colourful with roses, violets, fireweed and wild onions in bloom against a background of spruce forest and distant mountains. Four men on the tracking line were enough to haul the *Jupiter* along this stretch.

PLATE 17

PLATE 18

Trouble, when it did appear, was icy cold. Every now and then the crew "resting" on board would have to jump into the river and bodily haul the *Jupiter* off a gravel bar. When they reached the Franklin Mountains (a spur of the Rockies), the Bear River became a maze of islands and gravel bars divided by rapids and places of swift current. Here a field of ice stood like a wall along the shore. "We had to struggle along up to our thighs in that swift icy water with a whirl of rapids on one side and a sheer wall of ice on the other, often with precariously balanced overhanging masses of ice above our heads."

On the fourth day the water became so swift that the entire crew could not move the *Jupiter* upstream. The decision was made to lighten the big York boat by tracking some gear in the canoes. The biggest canoe, called the *Aldebaran,* was loaded with 1100 pounds and the smaller, *Polaris,* with 600. Douglas sent off five of the Indians with them, one steering in each canoe, one tracking the *Polaris* and two with the *Aldebaran.* "I watched them start with much misgiving and anxiety ..."

Douglas started this voyage expecting nothing but trouble from the Indians. His extensive reading of northern travellers had convinced him of the "thorough unreliability and inefficiency" of the Mackenzie River band. He watched them closely as they worked their way up the Bear River; their perseverance at the hard, steady job of tracking surprised him. He was pleasantly surprised to see his Indians return late in the afternoon of the same day with the news that they had got the two canoes safely up four miles of the river although they reported that conditions were very bad. "The opinion we had formed of the Northern Indians, generally, was certainly improved by our small personal experience with these men."

PLATE 18

PLATE 19

They sailed six miles across the bay to Fort Franklin, where Peter Dease in the winter of 1825-26 built a fort for Captain (later Sir) John Franklin who was making his second overland expedition to the Arctic coast. Of this fort, only a pile of chimney rocks now remained. A cluster of log shacks nearby belonged to Bear Lake Indians who came here for the excellent fishing.

Douglas sat up that night, "completely tired out" with the mosquitoes "in clouds," writing, "... the last letters that would reach civilization for more than a year." The Indians were eager to go back to Fort Norman at once; they actually started out at 1 a.m. At breakfast next morning the Douglas party saw the reason for their hurried departure. Coming across Bear Lake was the York boat of the Bear Lake Indians with Hornby and Father Rouvière aboard. The Bear Lakers had boasted they would beat the big, heavily-loaded *Jupiter* to the Lake. Douglas's Fort Norman Indians thought it would add a nice touch to greet the losers while heading *back* to Fort Norman.

PLATE 19

PLATE 20

On Sunday, July 16, they set out to sail the 195-mile length of Great Bear Lake. Rouvière and Hornby arrived at Franklin in time to watch them start. In 1911 the only maps existing for this immense 12,000 square-mile lake were Franklin's map drawn in 1828 and one made by the missionary, Father Petitot, in 1873. The population of Great Bear Lake in 1911 was reckoned at 200 Indians who lived nomadically, moving from one arm of the lake to another to hunt and fish.

François and his wife asked to stop at the settlement of log huts before leaving. They came back aboard with another little girl and another dog! The 55-foot *Jupiter* now had seven people and two dogs living aboard. The canoe, *Polaris,* was stowed upside down just forward of the mast, and provided a roof for the François family. The Douglas brothers and August Sandberg had quarters just aft of the mast. Here they hung two camp cots, one for Dr Sandberg and one for the brothers who kept watch alternately so were never asleep at once.

Great Bear Lake gave these newcomers a rough welcome. By 8 p.m. that first night, the great inland sea was riled by raw and threatening weather. By this time they were far out into the lake; the Indians stared wild-eyed and disbelieving at these three white men who chose open water in a storm. They, themselves, would have moved cautiously along the shore, sailing only when the wind was behind them. But Lionel Douglas was a sea-faring man, and George too had had experience on the open sea; all their instincts told them to avoid the dangers of an unknown shoreline.

Lionel took the tiller as the sea rose higher. He had not expected the *Jupiter* to sail well but she made even more leeway than he had feared. Their course lay eastward, down the length of the lake but they were being blown so far off course that by midnight the hills on the south side of the lake were visible. Lionel had another surprise when an island appeared to the north of them where no island was shown on their maps. Knowing how most travellers clung to the shoreline, it occurred to the Douglas brothers that they might be the first white people ever to see this island.

PLATE 20

PLATE 21

George tried to sleep from 8 to 12 p.m. but found himself chilled to the bone.   Now, as he took over from Lionel, mist filled the eerie half-light of the wild Arctic night, and the sea rose ever higher.

> ... the old *Jupiter* wallowed along through it, her timbers groaning and her sides swelling in and out like an accordion as the strain was thrown on and off the weather shrouds. I expected something to carry away any moment. Lion, who had turned in but who was sleeping no more than I had done, said afterward that he expected the whole side of the boat to give way. What François thought we never knew, probably his fears of a sudden end were partly compensated for by the feeling that his ideas were now shown to be right; and that our methods, carried out in spite of his protest, had been proved quite crazy.

At 2 a.m. the chilled and battered sailors sighted a long line of spruce trees on what appeared to be an island. It was a hook-shaped point of land, enclosing a large bay on the south coast. Two hours later, they sailed into it, thankful indeed for the quiet waters. "In fact we had struck the only place on this coast that was safe from a north wind."

George Douglas would say afterward that Great Bear had been kind to them. Providing shelter when they desperately needed it was perhaps her kindest gift. He and Lionel both doubted that the *Jupiter* could have held together much longer.

PLATE 21

PLATE 22

On the morning of July 20 after suffering greatly from cold and wet, they neared Gros Cap and sighted a York boat. They were delighted to land and meet Joe Hodgson "a fine-looking old man, a well-known old-timer in the North." He had wintered with his family on Dease Bay and was on his way out to civilization. Hodgson sold the use of his shack on the Dease River to the Douglas party for one tin of tobacco, a side of bacon and a bottle of brandy.

They got underway again only to spend four days hung up by fog. Finally on July 24 they got the wind they needed and the *Jupiter* "showed a capacity for speed quite unsuspected."

They were now heading for Big Island which guards the entrance to the Dease River. Elated by the speed of the *Jupiter,* they boomed along into the channel between island and shore, past the site of old Fort Confidence built by the Dease expedition in 1837. Four chimneys stood sentinel on a grassy space, surrounded by spruce trees. Near the site was a camp of Indians; "they were in the wildest state of excitement at our appearance and ran along the shore shouting and waving their arms." Next, the *Jupiter* ran past a small log shack which must have been Hornby's house.

> We sped across the beautiful bay behind Big Island with its rocky spruce-covered shores and rock islets; the nearer we got to the end of our journey the faster the *Jupiter* went; we entered the Dease River flying, regardless of possible sand-bars or shoals. On and on up the river we went in triumph; in spite of banks and bends the wind held fair and strong; the *Jupiter* never stopped in her wild career till she ran hard and fast aground on a gravel bar in mid-stream, just below the first rapid.

Their eight-day crossing was over. They had reached the long point formed by a horseshoe bend in the river, where Hodgson had built his shack. Here they would winter.

PLATE 22

PLATE 23

Four days after the *Jupiter's* race up the Dease River, two of the party were underway again. Lionel remained at Hodgson's Point to build their winter house. (The Hodgson shack was so poorly built that they had decided at once to build their own.)

In three busy days the Douglas brothers, August Sandberg, and François hauled out the *Jupiter*, developed all the photos taken so far, unpacked all their gear and re-packed a 50-day outfit for George Douglas and August Sandberg's attempt to reach the Coppermine River.

PLATE 24

To guide him, Douglas had a sketch map from the Canadian Geological Survey which was much at variance with the accounts of explorers. David Hanbury's account seemed to Douglas the most consistent and reliable but Hanbury had travelled in the opposite direction: "for him all roads led to Bear Lake, while ours was the more difficult task of ascending, with possible roads at the latter point branching out in all directions."

On the fifth day of uphill work they came to a high, flat-topped sandy hill where their guides let them down – the sketch map could not be connected with anything visible and Hanbury's notes led them to expect his Sandy Creek to come in from the north-east while they found only a stream from the west.

The Dease petered out into stony, gravelly streams. They tried Sandy Creek and found it also a rivulet. They walked four miles to a granite ridge and came back no less perplexed. They decided to push along Sandy Creek. Push and drag it was, haul, unload, portage, reload and haul again. When the stream branched, their indecision doubled. They tried the left branch but it veered west when they wanted to go east. So they made camp at the junction, determined to search out the Dismal Lakes on foot.

They struck across to Granite Ridge in weather that was thick, rainy, cold, raw and dotted with snow. When it became impossible to see in any direction, they sat under a high, rocky cliff, "cursing the country, cursing the weather, cursing Hanbury and his description (who didn't deserve it) ..."

Suddenly a big bull caribou came trotting directly toward them. They shot it. This was their first sighting of the legendary caribou said to move across the tundra in hundreds of thousands, in unbroken lines that would pass a man for days at a time. They skinned it, cut up the meat, piled it on a rock and covered it with the hide, appreciating the importance of this animal to the Indians and Inuit. It gave them nourishing food; hide for warm clothing, moccasins, tents and sleeping bags; sinews for thread; bones for needles, arrows and tools; and its skin could be stretched on to the frames of the Inuit kayaks.

When the weather cleared Douglas and Sandberg went on. At the end of the ridge they could see the Dease River coming out of a long lake to the east. They went back to camp and set out next day on the Dease again.

They were still five miles from Long Lake (later to be known as Lake Rouvière) when their river dwindled out. They went a distance on foot but could see no navigation ahead. Back at their canoe, surrounded by desolate waste, in a mood of failure, they made camp as the wind rose and struck them with a violent storm. "We called this place 'Camp Despair' and desperate indeed did our chances of success seem when we turned in that wild and stormy night."

The one chance remaining was to try Sandy Creek again. "About two miles above the point at which we had turned back before, we came on some features that made us think that this, after all, might have been Hanbury's route."

After three long days of incessant work, the mountains closed in around them; they had followed Sandy Creek to its source. Beyond was an opening through the mountains, a divide they hoped. On foot they went on and at the end of a long ridge, they sighted a long sheet of water ... the Dismal Lakes at last!

It was Thomas Simpson (brother of Sir George Simpson, Governor of the Hudson's Bay Company) who gave these lakes their name. In 1838 he surveyed this country with Peter Warren Dease, searching for a route to the Arctic coastline. Simpson wrote, "a height of land of six miles, north-north-east, led to a narrow chain of lakes, that wind for upwards of thirty miles in a south-easterly direction through a dismally barren, rocky country, producing not a tree or shrub, and seemingly unfrequented by any living creature."[1]

Douglas and Sandberg sat on one of the bare rocks above a sheet of water, still and dark as death, trapped between brooding hills. "Anything more unspeakably dismal than the western end I never saw; the lake is shut in by high bare rocky hills; those to the north still had huge drifts of snow in places, probably these drifts never disappear."

While Douglas sat thinking of Simpson's description of this land "unfrequented by any living creature," he suddenly snapped to attention. Moving on a hill about a mile away was a man. By the time he focused his binoculars on him, the stranger was disappearing over a hill. But the quick glimpse showed Douglas that the man was an Inuit. Quickly and cautiously, the two white men approached the hill, "highly excited at the prospect of meeting these people."

PLATE 25

Douglas and Sandberg managed to get quite close before the man saw them. "We threw up our arms calling out 'Teyma! Teyma!' about the only Eskimo word I knew. He did the same, his arms were fairly trembling with fright, and he kept repeating something over and over in a low moaning tone."

It was fortunate for their meeting that no Indian guides accompanied Douglas and Sandberg. The Inuit fear of the white man was the fear of the unknown; their fear of the Indian that of known treachery handed down in story and song from generation to generation. In 1771, at a place called Bloody Falls on the Coppermine River, Samuel Hearne watched in horror and disgust as Indians fell on and butchered an entire camp of Inuit who had come up from Coronation Gulf to fish for salmon. The vast region stretching east from Great Bear toward the Coppermine and north toward the coast was a sort of no-man's land where the meeting of Indian and Inuit took place at the dire peril of the weaker party.

Douglas and Sandberg did their best to reassure the frightened man. "He was a stoutly built man, about five feet four inches high. His hair hung straight and black behind, all the front part of it was cropped close to the skin. His face was open and intelligent, with rosy cheeks and a candidly engaging smile. He was dressed in caribou skins and sealskin boots, his general appearance was quite as clean as our own ..." Beside him were spears and a sealskin case which contained a bow and arrows and also a roll of skin set up on crossed sticks.

They attempted to talk to him using the Inuit name for the Dismal Lakes, "Teshierpi." He nodded and said, "Teshairping, Teshi-arping." Douglas had a small chunk of chocolate in his pocket and with gestures he offered it to the man. He hesitated, then cautiously put it in his mouth. "Presently an expression of intense delight passed over his face."

His manner became nervous and uneasy when they showed him by sign language that they wanted him to return to their canoes and help portage their stuff to Teshi-arping Lake. He agreed and they set out with him following, but before long he began to lag behind. When he was far back he turned, and Douglas and Sandberg could see him on the flat, bare terrain making "a bee-line back to his camp." There he gathered up his hunting gear and sped away toward the lake.

PLATE 26

It took two days to portage everything over the 6½ miles to the Dismal Lakes. In heavy rain they paddled 27 miles to the first narrows where they found the shore, "... strewn with the bones of caribou; bones of all ages scattered like driftwood along the beach." It was evident that Inuit regularly came here to hunt. Lines of stones set up on end were apparently used to direct the caribou toward their killers.

After breakfast next morning, on a brighter day, Douglas climbed a hill and discovered a camp. A kayak was set on a stone trestle and fur clothing lay about. Had the Inuit fled for fear of white men? Douglas and Sandberg put a few needles and files on the objects; under the kayak, they left a piece of milk chocolate as a kind of signature.

PLATE 24

PLATE 25

PLATE 26

PLATE 27

On the Kendall River they ran all day, down the rapid, boulder-jumbled river, until the strain of dodging rocks and veering off rock walls began to wear them down. "I can well remember my dismay later on in the afternoon ... to find ourselves at the head of a long, dangerous rapid full of big boulders. It was a regular hill, and we went down that place like a toboggan slide."

The Kendall finally ran into the Coppermine through a canyon walled with limestone cliffs. Here they struck a boulder which knocked a huge hole in the canoe. The impact swung them broadside into the "set." Douglas struggled to get the bow forward while Sandberg desperately shoved them off jagged rocks, "and we came through the canyon in triumph, running the canoe ashore on the beach below just before she sunk."

PLATE 28

It was a blessed relief to reach the smooth Coppermine River. Douglas felt pride and elation as well to have reached a goal set half in jest in a conversation a year-and-a-half ago with Cousin James one evening in his private railway car in Mexico. A lovely streak of sunlight lit up the opposite shore of the Coppermine River.

PLATE 27

PLATE 28

PLATE 29

While Douglas spent the next morning repairing his canoe, August Sandberg began at once to search for copper-bearing rocks. Then Douglas turned to another pressing need – food. When the two men met again that evening, Douglas had caribou steaks for their supper and Dr Sandberg had specimens of copper.

While they worked along the river, they often stood facing downstream, longing to follow it to the Arctic Sea. But time forbade. They spent only ten days on the Coppermine, arriving at the height of northern summer, the mosses and sedges and willows all green; but when they started up the Kendall again, summer was gone, "... scarcely a green leaf was to be seen. The mosses were every conceivable shade of red, wonderfully brilliant; the willows were a uniform bright yellow; the dwarf birches yellow also but paler and less brilliant; the sedges growing along the shore in the water were all mauve and cerise. It was the most beautiful display of colour in flora conceivable."

PLATE 29

PLATE 30

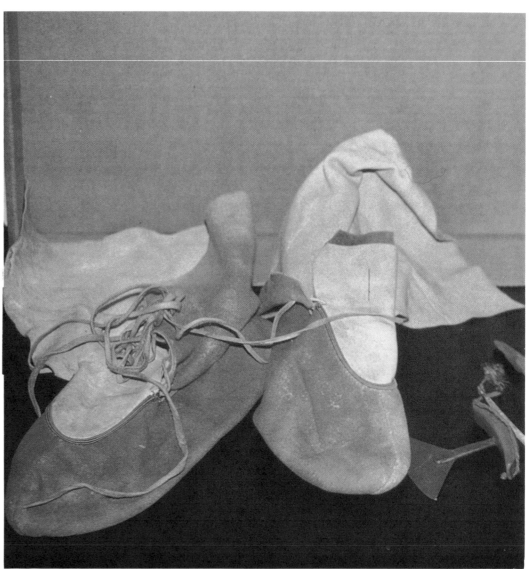

PLATE 30

On their return journey they spent two days storm-bound on the north shore of the middle Dismal Lake. Watching the gale blow out of the north-west, they marvelled at the sudden fury of this land which had been so benevolent a few days ago. It now became imperative to get over the divide before the waters turned to ice.

At the narrows they checked the Inuit camp and found that people had been there. The needles and files were gone and the kayak moved. "It was very tantalising to find such traces of them but not to see the Eskimos themselves ..."

At their old camp site at the junction of Sandy Creek and the Dease, they had left a cache of food in a waterproof canvas bag hung on a cross-arm between two small trees. When Douglas took down the bag, he found it tied up in a way that was strange to him. He opened the bag and found a small sealskin coat and a pair of sealskin slippers – gifts from the Inuit. Also in the bag were arrows with spruce shafts, copper-tipped bone heads and some tiny objects carved out of ivory.

No gift from the south could have provided the thrill of these beautiful objects from a people who were, in every sense of the word, strangers to Douglas and Sandberg. A whole year passed before they learned what the ivory trinkets were for: one was to pierce the nose of marmots to carry them; the other, a handle with sinew attached, was for carrying the stomachs of caribou. (These gifts from the Inuit are now at Trent University in Peterborough.)

PLATE 31

On September 11, they reached home, straining their eyes for the house they hoped to see. They ran the last rapid and then they saw it, "looking exceedingly neat and trim." Lionel saw them through the window where he was papering the inside with magazines he had got from Hornby.

It was a joyful celebration, a treat to sit at a real table and eat the supper Lionel prepared. The house was spacious, ship-shape, snug and bright; Lionel had built with pride and care.

PLATE 31

Chapter 6
Frozen in Place

Dease Bay, the remote north-eastern arm of Great Bear Lake, was a busy place in the fall and winter of 1911. On July 24 a small group of Bear Lake Indians, encamped near old Fort Confidence, watched the flamboyant entrance of the Douglas party as the *Jupiter* flew across the bay and careened up the river with the wind at its back. Then, on July 29, Rouvière, who was travelling with Bear Lake Indians in a York boat, arrived and moved into Hornby's cabin near the old fort ruins. Rouvière and Hornby came up the Bear River behind the Douglas party, arriving at Franklin one day later. Then, while Rouviere went on in the York boat, Hornby waited at Franklin for Joe Hodgson whose boat he needed to move his supplies. He finally reached Dease Bay on August 10. An impatient Rouvière was waiting for him. Two days later they started up the Dease to seek the Inuit. Douglas and Sandberg were ahead of them, having a terrible time in the confusing headwaters of the Dease River.

Thus the Douglas party and the Rouvière party became winter neighbours on the Dease and fellow travellers in the Barrens beyond Great Bear. On their fall trips both parties were engaged in a race against time to get back to the mouth of the Dease and to be frozen in for the winter in their chosen places.

It was September 20 before the two parties made contact. By this time Douglas and Sandberg were back from their brief look at the Coppermine and George had gone out again with Lionel to hunt and explore in the area of Observation Hill. Returning along the river, they met Hornby and heard of his and the Father's adventures.

Like Douglas and Sandberg, Hornby and Rouvière had had a hard struggle. They failed to find the Dismal Lakes and they set up camp on Lake Imaerinik at the headwaters of the Dease (Rouvière called it Dease Lake but Douglas renamed it Lake Rouvière). There they found the Inuit. From Hornby, Douglas heard of Rouvière's excitement: Hornby was carrying exuberant letters from Rouvière to Bishop Breynat and Father Ducot.

In October when Hornby returned to Lake Imaerinik to bring Rouvière back, the Douglas brothers went with him. They were disappointed to find that the Inuit who had been there for many weeks had all gone the day before, heading north to the sea coast for the winter.

Douglas found the location of the cabin on Lake Rouvière rather dismal. "That part of the country was bad enough in summer; in early winter with the sun only a short distance above the horizon and the air full of frozen mist the outlook was miserable indeed." But there was nothing miserable about its chief inhabitant. Rouvière described his first meeting with the Inuit with great éclat. After two days of searching on the Barrens, he and Hornby met two Indians who reported Inuit in the direction they were heading. They marched on:

... for about a hour and a half. Nothing, nothing at all. ... Suddenly the idea comes to me to go back on my tracks. Mr Hornby doesn't altogether share my idea: he decides to go on farther. So I go back on my tracks. After walking about three quarters of an hour, I see on the top of a hill three living things. Are they caribou? Are they men? I can't tell at that distance. To make sure I go towards the hill. After walking about ten minutes, I see a crowd of people on the blind side of the hill. There's no doubt about it: these are Eskimo. Thanks, O Mary. A main point of my mission is about to be fulfilled. O Mother, pray bless my steps and make this meeting fruitful. ... one of them stops the front ones and comes towards me, raising his arms to the sky and leaning his head to the right, then bowing his whole body to the ground. He does this several times over. At first I don't make any sign; but seeing that he goes on and on repeating the same gestures, I reply simply by lifting my arms to the sky. From a distance I notice that his pace increases and that all the others rush to join him. It was their sign of greeting to show that these are trustworthy people. When he was close enough to recognise me, he stopped for a moment, then turning towards his companions, cried out to them in quite a loud voice: 'Krablunar' (Kabloona) ... that is, a Whiteman. Then he increases his pace and reaches me smiling and holding out his hand. Immediately he takes me by the arm to present me to all the rest. I was wearing my cassock and carrying my Oblate cross. This latter strikes them at once. They look at it and I try by signs to tell them that he who is on this cross was killed for us. At once I give them some medals which I pass around by hand. Instantly everybody surrounds me, swamping me with questions or requests. I try to make them understand that I have come to stay among them. Immediately they all want to come with me to bring back my gear, so that I can stay with them. One of them came with me as far as my tent which we reached about two o'clock in the morning.[1]

The Douglases stayed only a few days at Lake Rouvière, then they headed home, hunting on the way. The Father travelled back separately with the Indian boy, Harry, the son of Hornby's companion, Arimo. Hornby stayed at Lake Rouvière to try some trapping.

It was during the winter that they all got to know each other. In spite of the cold and dark, it was a special time made easy by a sense of satisfaction – Douglas had reached his Coppermine, Rouvière had met his Inuit – but also made exciting by anticipation of the greater challenge ahead, the search for copper deposits and the saving of souls.

Douglas admired Rouvière's single-minded awareness of mission; he also marvelled at his ability to endure physical hardship. George and Lionel each spent one winter night in the crude

Hornby cabin near Fort Confidence and nearly froze to death. Rouvière and Hornby got no caribou that winter and seldom tried to hunt ptarmigan; they existed on dried meat obtained from the Indians and lake trout caught through a hole in the ice. Through that long winter there was never a word of complaint from Rouvière about these living conditions.

Nevertheless, Rouvière and Hornby came often to share the good life in the snug Douglas cabin. On Christmas Day, the five white men dined in style with Arctic hare for dinner, followed by plum pudding. For supper they had smoked caribou tongues, the great delicacy of the North, of which Father Rouvière was particularly fond. Douglas realized that Rouvière was not oblivious to comfort and enjoyment as Hornby seemed to be, just more able than most men to forgo such pleasures in favour of a larger goal.

In return for warm shelter and a good meal the two visitors provided the "society" which helped them all to withstand the long dark Arctic winter. Talk took them around the world. August Sandberg talked of his Swedish homeland, and of remote Mexican places where he and George had worked together. The Douglas brothers shared memories of their beloved Northcote Farm in Ontario. Jean-Baptiste Rouvière reminisced about his native France and about Mende in Lozère where he was born in 1881. Hornby, sitting cross-legged on the floor talked in his educated English accent of the estate named Parkfield where he was born into a wealthy cotton-spinning family, of his years at Harrow where he excelled at sports, of Germany where he trained for the diplomatic service. He never made it very clear why he had come to Canada. Whatever importance his background had, it was obvious that the real interest of his life lay not in civilization, but here in this barren land.

The five men talked about rivers and routes and methods of travel, of Indian rumours and meetings with Inuit. Father Rouvière in particular, liked to turn the conversation to the Inuit – they were his grand mission, his raison d'être. He discussed the letter he was writing to Father Ducot and talked about the ten or twelve families who had been with him at Lake Rouvière:

All of them seem quite well disposed, and if I could manage to learn their language a little, I have plenty of hope in them. There will be some thick heads among them, I think, but I don't think these will be the majority. They are too good-hearted to reject [withstand] grace. But the language ... I have collected some words, but not as many as I could wish ...

In the Douglas cabin, Rouvière could not put into words that he blamed Hornby for his lack of time to learn the language. But in his letter to Father Ducot he made it clear:

[A]nd that ... I must say frankly ... is Mr Hornby's fault for leaving me alone for about a month. Having to finish ... or practically to build ...the house, I have had only a little time to devote to them. For all that I am quite satisfied, for I now know the country a little and the ordinary places where they are to be found. If next year Monseigneur is pleased to send me among them again, I shall be able to stay with them at least two whole months before they move off towards the sea. Actually I am ... to say truth ... on holiday ....[2]

Hornby was having a good holiday too. If he ever really enjoyed life it was probably during this winter of 1911-12. He was like a child playing with danger and loving it. The Douglas party, masters at planning, at foresight, at taking care, were there like parents to offer support if the game got out of hand. Pictures of him on the Barrens with the Douglas party in the spring of 1912 show an aura of happiness which never really came again.

Often these winter discussions turned to the man Hornby called Stevenson (Vilhjalmur Stefansson) and how he had come overland from the Coppermine River in August of 1910. Hornby said he travelled with the Inuit and lived like them, wore their clothing and ate their food. Stefansson told him that the Inuit he met on Cape Bexley and Victoria Island had never seen white men. Hornby said Stefansson had built a cabin on the upper Dease and wintered there last year before disappearing with the Inuit.

As the five men talked in the Arctic winter of 1911-12, Stefansson was as unknown to the world as themselves. Not until the fall of 1912 did he reach the South (about the same time as Douglas) and give to the press his news about the "Copper Eskimos." To the fact that they were a people untouched by the 200 years of civilization to the south of them, Stefansson added mystery. Why did these men look so much more European than other Inuit if they were not of European descent? A reporter dubbed them "Blond Eskimos" and they – as well as Vilhjalmur Stefansson – became front page news.

Without suspecting what a drama these Inuit were about to provide for the outside world, the little party in Lionel's snugly-built house on the Dease was eager to meet them again in the spring.

PLATE 32

The population on the Dease at the east end of Great Bear Lake in the winter of 1911-12 consisted of 5 white men and about 25 Indians.

During the fall the Douglas party got to know the Indians before they all moved west to hunt. Old Jacob was "... the chief favourite and most welcome at our house... the only one of the men who would condescend to smile and look happy." He was also the most fluent in the sign language by which they communicated. But one day when he looked mournful and his gestures were wild and weird, they could make no sense of his signs. "It was sometime later before I knew ...he had had a row with his wife, and wished me to go and smooth things out!"

Another favourite was "... the Indian woman who worked for Hornby, and her family; I think she was a widow, I never knew her name. She was a cheery energetic woman, quite as effective a worker as any of the men and a whole lot more cheerful. She had a boy of about fourteen, Harry we called him, who was a nice lad."

PLATE 33

Jean-Baptiste Rouvière was a quiet, dedicated man. He had the look of a man still young but already wise, with lines of worry between his serious black eyes, as if he somehow knew himself marked for martyrdom. He was content during the winter of 1911 because he had already established his outpost mission on Lake Imaerinik and looked forward to converts in the spring. He was good company and well-liked by both the Douglas brothers and Sandberg.

PLATE 33

PLATE 34

Hornby provided the perfect contrast to Father Rouvière. Worry of any sort was alien to him; he never thought of tomorrow. His conversation, like his life-style, was often erratic, sometimes pointless; yet he could talk of a cultured English home and hearth so far removed from this one that it seemed another world.

PLATE 34

PLATE 35

The Camp at old Fort Confidence was built in 1837 by the Dease and Simpson expedition and was their quarters for two winters. In 1848 it was rebuilt and used by Sir John Richardson and Dr Rae during their search for the lost Sir John Franklin.

Near here was the house where Hornby and Father Rouvière wintered. The accommodation was miserable. Lionel nearly froze during the one night he spent there, trying to sleep on the floor. George also spent a night there and since he packed a thermometer, he found the temperature 2° below Fahrenheit on the floor and 7° above near the beams. For each of the Douglas brothers once was enough at the Hornby cabin, but Hornby and Rouvière often came to stay in the warmth and comfort of the Douglas-Sandberg place.

PLATE 36

When Hornby went back to Lake Rouvière in late October with dogs and sleds to bring the Father out, George and Lionel went along to gain experience of winter travel. The trip in was a positive pleasure. On the return journey they decided to haul their own sleds while Rouvière brought out the dog-team and Hornby stayed behind to do some trapping. They learned some terrible truths about sled-hauling. One night they were "so completely done up" from pulling the short, heavy, awkward sleds that they could neither pitch a tent nor light a fire. Three miles from home they had to abandon one toboggan. Lionel with a hurt knee, George with a pulled sinew in his instep, the two brothers walked painfully home.

Dr Sandberg then went out enthusiastically to haul in the abandoned toboggan and found that he hated the sport as much as the other two. Often, during the long winter, the three men laughed about their foolish attempt to man-haul the sleds.

PLATE 35

PLATE 36

PLATE 37

PLATE 37

Their winter regime was probably the most organized and agreeable ever spent by white men in the Arctic.

One is reminded of the men of Franklin's expedition who dined on silver and lived in style while ice-bound in Victoria Strait, only to scatter their silver spoons along a trail of death as they tried to outwalk starvation. The Douglas comfort and style was of a different sort – homespun but calculated, utilitarian, well-engineered, imported from civilization but adapted and attuned to the rigors of this North by a careful weighing of all the odds.

The house was built of spruce logs, chinked with moss and caribou hair, mudded inside and out and papered inside with magazine pages. The floor was made of wooden blocks set on end with sand to fill the cracks. The roof of small spruce poles was caulked with caribou hair topped with dry sand, then covered with a waterproof canvas.

PLATE 38

The fireplace was wide and the chimney drew well. Ventilation was controlled by holes bored in the door and fitted with removable wooden plugs. The house was snug and warm.

On September 25 the Douglas party divided their duties into cooking, wood-chopping and hunting, which they rotated by the week. Meals were arranged so that the hunter and wood-chopper could take best advantage of the little daylight available. Breakfast was at 9:30 a.m., dinner at 3:30 p.m., supper at 8 p.m.

> For breakfast we had oatmeal porridge; occasionally bacon and beans, but more often some kind of hash made of caribou or ptarmigan with desiccated potatoes, bannock, and tea. Dinner consisted of soup; caribou steaks or stews, or roast ptarmigan, with desiccated potatoes; bannock and stewed apples. Supper was simply bannock and chocolate.

PLATE 38

PLATE 39

Christmas was celebrated in great style with Father Rouvière and Hornby in attendance. Their pièce de résistance was an Arctic hare, the only one seen all winter. Lionel, who was cook that week, produced a plum pudding served with blueberry jam which he had made in summertime. After dinner they had Teshierpi Toddy (a drink made of brandy and desiccated raspberries first used to celebrate their arrival at the Dismal Lakes) and a game of 'twenty-one' using squares of chocolate for stakes.

By Christmas time the temperature was so low that the spruce tree trunks were frozen and moved with a jerky motion when the wind blew. (The coldest weather was between January 9 and 14 when the readings were between -51° and -59° Fahrenheit. The sun was not visible from their house from November 26 to January 9.)

When the 3:30 meal was over, a roaring fire secured them from the cold, a second candle burned against the darkness, and conversation pushed back the isolation of vast empty space.

"Our Xmas Party. Left to Right: Lion, Father Rouvière, the Doctor, Myself."

PLATE 39

PLATE 40

In January Hornby and Sandberg attempted to go to Fort Norman for the mail but found themselves unable to withstand the Arctic winds and cold. After they turned back, life in the two cabins settled into frozen routine. Here George sits by the table in their crowded quarters.

PLATE 41

The hunter of the week usually left the cabin by 11 a.m. to make a ten to fifteen mile tramp in search of game. Caribou were extremely scarce. At the end of November, a small herd came near Hodgson's Point and they got six in two days. These, alternating with ptarmigan, supplied their fresh meat throughout the winter. Lionel was the outstanding hunter of the party. Accurate and quick and a patient stalker of ptarmigan, he kept a line of twenty (sometimes fifty) plucked and frozen birds hanging between two trees. "Our best friends in that country were the dead spruce trees and the ptarmigan."

The dead spruce trees were the vocation of the weekly wood-chopper who would spend two days chopping down and hauling trees on a toboggan, and the next days sawing and splitting. Each wood-chopper tried to keep a stock-pile of logs by the house in case of bad weather. George's stock grew very large, and he wrote in *Lands Forlorn* two years later, "... it jars on me yet to think of some of those fine logs that I hauled in with such care and labour used by Father Rouvière and Hornby the following winter."

The cook had duties besides cooking. He brought water from a hole kept open in the river while ice around it froze six feet thick. He brought wood in from outside and cleaned the cabin. Then he could attend to his own washing, mending and sewing.

PLATE 40

PLATE 41

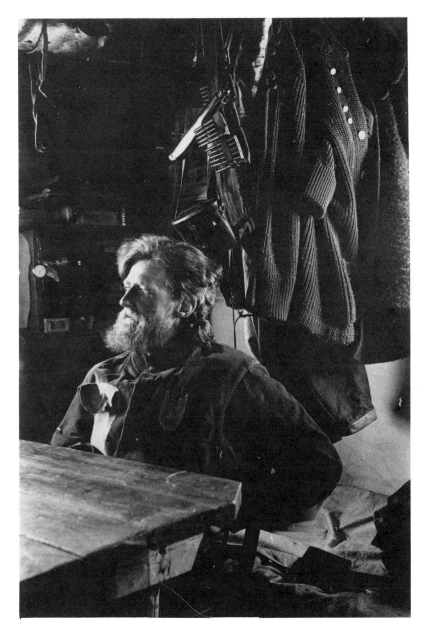

PLATE 42

In early February Indians began drifting back to Hodgson's Point. They had suffered privation and lost some of their dogs to starvation. In late February they decided to make their annual journey to Fort Norman for supplies. They left on the 27th with Hornby carrying Father Rouvière's letters to Father Ducot and Bishop Breynat. In the letter written the day before they left, a new note of uncertainty crept in with the missionary's news:

> Another question ... and this is a little embarrassing. Mr Hornby passionately wants me to go out to the sea in April. On the other hand, I daren't say too much against him, because I want to go with him myself ... but I thought we should be able to go there in March and this becomes impossible. If you could use a little influence on Mr Hornby to dissuade him from this journey to the sea or express disapproval of my going with him, several things would be simplified.[1]

Douglas was aware of the priest's worries. They all talked about the timing of a spring trip to the coast. He understood Rouvière's growing concern that Hornby's sense of timing might not suit his own.

PLATE 43

On March 24 the Indians returned without Hornby. They had a team of dogs for Father Rouvière and instructions from Father Ducot that he should return to Fort Norman. An Indian would travel with him and Hornby would come back with that guide.

> The Father left on March 28th. We were sorry to say good-bye to him. He had added greatly to the pleasure of our life in winter quarters, and it was with sincere regret that we saw him off on his journey back to the Mission.

The long winter on the Dease was almost over.

PLATE 42

PLATE 43

PLATE 44

As the sun brightened and the days stretched, an eagerness to travel tugged at the Douglas party. With the help of François and his dogs, they began staging most of their gear to the Father's house on Lake Rouvière.

PLATE 45

Hornby returned from Fort Norman on April 17 with two more dogs, all he could get. On April 30 the grand start was made. They had two toboggans with three dogs to each.

On their second day out, they sighted a herd of several hundred caribou. George and Lionel shot three. Harry and the dogs were both in a state of great excitement. "Cutting up caribou was Harry's particular delight; he always used to appropriate for himself the bones of the fore legs and crack them for the marrow." The dogs, who had all endured various degrees of starvation, ate until they could eat no more.

PLATE 45

PLATE 46

Fourteen-year-old Harry joined the party on the night before they left. He travelled with Hornby so that the two of them could go off on their own if they wished.

Harry shared their last "civilized" meal at Hodgson's Point. He was very solemn, trying to eat hominy with a fork, "...plainly contemptuous of white men and their ways, especially their food." But once on the trail, Harry found himself at home and happy. It was especially satisfying to George that this Indian boy who considered all white men stupid and foolish – with the exception of Hornby – eventually approved of the Douglas party, "... and I think ended in even admiring us!"

PLATE 46

PLATE 47

From Lake Rouvière on, their gear amounted to four toboggan loads. This meant they had to cover the distance twice. By May 8 they had moved everything to Teshierpi Mountain about four miles from the narrows between the second and third Dismal Lakes. Dr Sandberg stayed there to begin geological work while the others hauled the first load overland in what they hoped was a straight line to the Coppermine.

At 2 a.m. they stopped for lunch on a little patch of dry ground where dry spruce was available for a big fire. "In high spirits we sat before that cheerful blaze and filled up on caribou; enthusiastic over sledge journeys, overnight travelling, over the country, and most of all over caribou liver." A few miles farther on, they sighted the westerly bend of the Coppermine.

Hornby went back for Sandberg. By the time they arrived, the weather was mild again, the snow disappearing on the levels. The warm weather misled George into thinking the Coppermine might break up, and he began to build a canoe frame using the toboggan which he carefully broke up into thin strips. These were carefully lashed together with *babiche* and electric insulating tape. A silk tarpaulin covered the frame.

Harry was much impressed; "...he said that he supposed white men couldn't make anything unless they had a hammer and nails, and he started to make a funny little model to take back and show the other Indians how we had built a canoe of our sleighs."

When they did move north on the Coppermine on May 24, it was on foot using both dogs and humans as pack animals. Strong gales out of the north-west stopped the boat-building and threatened to blow away their exposed camp.

The best of the dogs could carry more than 50 pounds. Hornby, the smallest man among them, could carry an amazing weight, and once packed a load of caribou meat that weighed 225 pounds.

They moved slowly, prospecting along the way, the spruce trees dwindling until they disappeared, the parallel ranges of basalt hills becoming lower as they moved down from the Coppermine Mountains toward the sea.

PLATE 47

PLATE 48

They made their northernmost camp at Bloody Falls where the river cuts through basalt rock walls, violent in its narrow channel, a crooked, raging rapid dropping fifteen feet in three hundred yards. It was impossible to stand here and not picture the terrible massacre for which this place was named.

But when the Douglas party discovered the Inuit on the far bank, there was joy on both sides, and they were greeted with cries of "Teyma. Teyma!"

The Coppermine was at last breaking up and ice had jammed at the lower part of the rapids. Two of the Inuit decided to cross on this ice bridge although it might be swept away at any moment by the clear water above. There were about thirty Inuit now on the high east bank watching, mostly women and children, one of them visibly afraid that her man would be drowned. One of the men went back to bring across a musk-ox skin; a third man returned with him.

It was a delight to meet these vivacious, well-bred people ... We could carry on a conversation only by signs ...

They explained that they had come to spear salmon, giving a most comical imitation of a fish wriggling at the end of a spear. As soon as the flies came they were going inland to hunt caribou; and the representation they gave of a man pestered by mosquitoes, slapping his face and neck, was extremely realistic; one could almost hear the mosquitoes buzzing....

We wanted also to find out where they picked up the pieces of native copper used by them for their weapons and utensils; they pointed to the south and gave a ludicrous representation of a man bending under a heavy load to typify a long journey, finally struggling up a steep hill and arriving quite exhausted. ...

They went back to get some more musk-ox skins, of which we understood they had seven altogether at their camp; they had scarcely crossed before the whole ice jam carried away and we had no further intercourse with them.

PLATE 48

PLATE 49

"At last after a weary nine-mile walk from the Bloody Falls we stood on the very edge of the continent." From the beach of sand and mud, they walked on to the smooth and solid ice of the Arctic Ocean waving the flags which they had carried four thousand miles for this purpose.

The brief ceremony was over. "It was Homeward Bound! now, our faces were turned south again at last; a retreat ever southward, of which the end was five long months and many thousands miles away."

PLATE 49

COPPERMINE • 97

PLATE 50

Three miles from the sea, they again met Inuit, this time a family of five. Their easy manners and well-bred ways soon had the Douglas brothers completely charmed. They seemed a "highly civilized and cultivated people" who had never seen a book and had no concept of written words. George had copied a few words from the dictionary made by Father Emile Petitot. Most of these they did not understand but when he did hit upon one of their words, their astonishment knew no bounds.

George's notebook was a magic thing to them. The oldest girl, about twelve or thirteen, was particularly delighted when he let her make marks in it.

When it came to the matter of food, gracious manners did not quite bridge their cultural differences. George and Lionel although both very hungry, looked at "...that slimy repulsive mess of luke-warm oil, blood and half-raw meat ..." and could not tackle it. They declined as gracefully as they could.

The brothers asked them whether the family had met Stefansson but could not make them understand. They had a sheet-metal trough and tin pots but these may have come from Captain Joe Bernard who had brought his ship, *Teddy Bear*, to Coronation Gulf soon after Stefansson's visit of 1910.

PLATE 50

PLATE 51

As they left the Inuit and crossed the ridge to their own campsite, it was midnight with the sun still on the horizon. "...marvellous mirages transformed the rocky coast line to vague enchanted shapes; a fairy land of gold, crimson, and mother-of-pearl ..."

We started southward again next morning, it was almost a matter of regret to do so; I should have liked nothing better than to have spent the summer with the Eskimos and become familiar with them, but this was quite out of the question under our circumstances.

As they moved south, the weather was fine, the ground was dry and the sun never set. They even found a level grassy point and spruce trees for a campsite which they named "Camp Comfort."

PLATE 51

When they came again to their "Teshierpi Camp" site, Lionel went hunting, met two Inuit and invited them back.

Harry puffed himself up with importance and began to cook for them. For northern Indians and Inuit to share food together was truly an historic moment and the boy may have realized this far more clearly than the white men who lacked the legacy of fear and hatred between the two races.

The Inuit liked the bacon raw but did not like it cooked. They enjoyed tea but when they tried sugar, they found it disagreeable.

Their families were camped nearby and were anxious to trade but the Douglas party could not carry any more gear. The women particularly wanted forks – not to eat with, but to use as combs. Photographs astonished them and they seemed to be most intrigued with the thinness of the image. It seemed unimportant to them whether the picture was held upside down or rightside up.

PLATE 56

A back view of the Inuit. The Douglas party felt that these people lacked the good looks and intelligence of the family group met on the Coppermine.

PLATE 52

PLATE 53

PLATE 54

PLATE 55

PLATE 56

PLATE 57

At their camp they had a small wedge tent made of caribou skin with the hair left on and a kayak frame. Douglas guessed that they had taken the covering off to carry it more easily in the wind.

PLATE 58

From Lake Rouvière, George and Lionel travelled in Hornby's leaky canoe with most of the gear while the other three walked with the dogs.

Their last day on the Dease River was warm and beautiful. As they soaked in the sunshine, they recalled the contrasts. They had travelled here in late fall, painfully hauling toboggans, a sense of "darkness, desolation and death" surrounding them. They had come here again on a luckless hunting trip when the temperature was -50° Fahrenheit. Now they saw the Barrens ablaze with flowers, all life triumphant with summertime: "... the grass and the willows were greener than ever, and the dwarf birches more delicately beautiful. The muskrats were alert and jubilant; geese flew overhead, ducks circled at every bend, and ptarmigan ashore chirped to their just hatched little ones; on every side there was activity and exultation."

PLATE 59

At Hodgson Point their house was half-lost among leafy willows, surrounded by green spruce and big blue flowers: "... we landed on the point that we had left buried under snow and ice and walked up to the house, perfectly stunned by the strangeness and difference of things."

They had only a few days to stay here, time to develop pictures, varnish the canoe which would carry their reduced load home, time to sort and select. Hornby planned to remain and to use some of the supplies they were leaving. Father Rouvière planned to return with another priest, use the Douglas house, and look after their equipment. They themselves hoped to return in the summer of 1913.

Their final good-byes to Hornby, to Harry, to the François family, to the dogs and even to the house, were surprisingly hard. Had they known that they would never see this spot again, leaving might have been harder still.

PLATE 57

PLATE 58

PLATE 59

PLATE 61

PLATE 60

The journey across Great Bear Lake began in the *Aldebaran*, a Peterborough canoe bought in Edmonton but built just twelve miles from Northcote Farm. On the journey north it had behaved well on the swift Athabasca.

The *Aldebaran* was 18'6" long with a 42" beam, and 18" deep. She was made of basswood strips with ribs close together for strength. Her sail had been made a year earlier by George and Lionel as they travelled down the Mackenzie on the *Grahame*. Her mast was from a small fire-killed spruce that they had cut at Smith's Landing, a tough piece of wood that would bend like a whip before this voyage was over.

PLATE 61

As they moved out beyond Big Island, they found the main body of the lake solid with ice. Their frail craft faced a strong north-east wind as they worked their way along the narrow stretch of open water near shore. All trace of summer had been left behind on the Dease, mosquitoes being the only fore-runners of warm weather here.

On the desolate north shore near the Haldane River, ice jammed against the land and they were held there for an entire week before they could move on.

Again, where Smith Bay narrows to 20 miles, they were unable to cross because of ice. As the days of July wore away with waiting, they began to be concerned that they could not catch the steamer, *Mackenzie River*. It was due to leave Fort Norman at the beginning of August. If they missed it, they would have to get out by way of the Yukon and Porcupine Rivers, or track their canoe up more than 900 miles (1500 km) of river system to Athabasca Landing.

PLATE 62

PLATE 62

At last they were able to move. It was July 16 when they finally rounded Gros Cap "... reefed down with our mast bending like a reed and the boat buried to the gunwales in foam."

Now the July winter was left behind; in Keith Arm the ice was gone and cold misery was replaced by halcyon days. When they moved out of Great Bear Lake, the current of the Bear River swept them along at an astonishing speed. They were now so anxious to catch the steamer that they travelled on into the night after a long, hard day.

PLATE 63

At 2 a.m. they came upon a large camp; ... "the whole outfit was here; Father Rouviere, Father Le Roy [LeRoux], Johnny Sanderson, and Jimmie Soldat, and the rest of the Indians." They roused up Johnny and Father Rouvière and learned the sad truth that the *Mackenzie River* had sailed south the Monday before.

There was no race to be won now so they made camp, cooked up pemmican and invited the Fathers to feast and visit. Hungry for news of the outside world, they were shocked to hear of the sinking of the *Titanic*. (Douglas learned later that his former employer, Benjamin Guggenheim of the Power and Mining Machinery Company, went down with the ship.)

Rouvière, after a spring and early summer at Fort Good Hope, was heading back to the Barrens and his beloved Inuit. With him he had a companion appointed specifically to solve the language problem. He was Father Guillaume LeRoux, a 27-year-old priest who had been at Fort Good Hope since 1907 and had mastered the language of the Mackenzie Basin Inuit.

Father Rouvière was eager to hear about the Douglas encounters with Inuit at Bloody Falls and near the Dismal Lakes. It should have been a happy occasion but the reaction of Father LeRoux marred it. Although the Douglas party had never met the new priest before, all three men felt that he intensely disliked them. True, they had awakened him in the middle of the night, but this was the North. Did he expect them to pass silently in the sub-Arctic night and lose a chance to visit which might never come again?

As the two parties sat up and talked until 4 a.m., George sized up the priests' outfit and become uneasy for them and for Hornby. Rouvière, LeRoux and Jimmy Soldat travelling together had a heavy load in their canoe and said they had not been able to bring Hornby any of the supplies he asked for. The Fathers were to live in the Douglas house and to have supplies which Douglas had left. Hornby, alone in his cabin near Fort Confidence, would run short. This promised trouble for the long winter ahead.

In the morning George actually put in writing that Hornby should have 200 pounds of food from the Douglas larder. Even as he wrote, he realized the awkwardness of the arrangement as the priests would be living in the house and would very likely run short themselves. The attitude of Father LeRoux added to his uneasiness.

At 10 a.m. George, Lionel and August Sandberg saw the missionary party off.

PLATE 64

Their arrival at Fort Norman was not at all what they expected. After all, they had made a 12-month, 400-mile journey fraught with danger, and had survived. No-one seemed to care.

The first people they saw, two priests, did not bother to return their greeting, in fact turned their backs. Hodgson and his son, another old trapper and the factor of the Northern Trading Company, did come and help them unload their gear. They had expected to be entertained and lauded at the HBC Post; instead Leon Gaudet waited until they had set up camp, then came to be entertained by them: "... we could even produce a bottle of cognac to celebrate the occasion!"

Laughing about it afterward, the three travellers realized that the northern explorer should reach the first outpost of civilization, "... ragged and half-starved, eating his moccasins and mitts." They failed to fit the picture.

PLATE 63

PLATE 64

PLATE 65

Perhaps another factor was involved in the low-key reception of the Douglas party. The North rarely made heroes of her own. This family birch bark canoe loaded with all the belongings of an Indian family, symbolized the precarious existence of the native people. Each winter some starved and some didn't. The little post of Fort Norman accepted survival or death as normal and made very little fuss over either. Only in the south would the travels of the Douglas-Sandberg party take on the proportions of an epic adventure.

PLATE 65

PLATE 66

If their arrival was less than dramatic, so was their departure. It involved long weeks of waiting. The *Mackenzie River* had been expected back on August 1. By mid-August the question was not only "when" but "if." If she did not come at all, they had to face the Yukon route with no way of knowing whether they would have help on the 80-mile portage to the Porcupine River.

They made a decision to start down the Mackenzie on August 21 if the steamer had not arrived by then. She came on August 17.

The *Mackenzie River* took them to Fort Smith. The steamer *Grahame* had already gone up-river from Smith's Landing but they had their own *Aldebaran* which would get them to Fort Chipewyan.

There they waited a week for the tug *Primrose* to come from Fond du Lac at the eastern end of Lake Athabasca. On September 13 they began the last part of their journey on the HBC scow, pulled by the tug.

PLATE 67

All was well until they laid up the *Primrose,* built in Peterborough 1894, for the winter at Fort MacKay. Now only muscle-power on a tracking line would move the overloaded scow upstream. The Indian pilot, a hard-worker himself, had no control over his men. The HBC officers who were on the scow, "... never interfered in any way and the outfit moved or stopped at the sweet will of the tracking crew."

PLATE 66

PLATE 67

PLATE 68

PLATE 68

Above Fort McMurray, the 150 miles of difficult and dangerous rapids were a test of Douglas's patience. The language in *Lands Forlorn* reveals the frustration built up over the 17 days it took to reach Pelican Portage: "... it was thoroughly humiliating to be so completely dependent on the pleasure of an unorganized bunch of hand-to-mouth half-breeds." An entry from his diary show us the pattern of a typical day:

Tuesday, Sept. 24th: Cold this morning; we had several degrees of frost last night and the mud near the water frozen. All hands had breakfast, then we hauled the scow a little farther up; there is a small cascade and we lightened the scow just below it. ...

Carried the stuff up about a quarter of a mile, loaded up and made a start again at 10 a.m. Stopped 10:15 to change heavy line for a light one; we were then at a comparatively quiet stretch of the river. The men had dinner here and we made a start again at 10:52. Stuck at 11, on again 11:15, stuck again at once, and fooled around till 12. We crossed the river then and had lunch on the other side. Water very shallow along here, constantly sticking and making scarcely any headway at all. From 1 till 2:30 nothing doing, then the men had tea.

Made a start again at 3:00 and attempted to go outside a shallow bar; the line broke and the scow drifted down to where it had been before tea; a hell of an outfit this is, unspeakably sloppy, the scow too small, no tracking line worth a damn, not enough men, and no one running things. We finally got up past Meatsu Point, then came a quiet stretch of the river for about a mile, then shallow water, and we stuck again. After fooling around for some time they decide to camp ...

But as usual – a little begrudgingly – Douglas gave the Indians credit where credit was due. "It was not till we were past the bad places that we were in the proper frame of mind to judge the performance of the crew, to give them just credit for their really hard work, and to realise how much wiser we had been in staying with the slow but safer scow."

PLATE 69

PLATE 69

The mood of the trip was lightened considerably by the company they had on board. Corporal "Denny" (Charles Deering) LaNauze of the Royal North West Mounted Police was on board bringing a crazy Indian woman from the Laird River out to Athabasca Landing. By the time Douglas and LaNauze shared the rigors and irritations of this journey, they had become close friends.

Even the mad woman added to the liveliness of the party. She was crazy in a pleasant way and would laugh, dance and sing. No-one could speak her language and one could only guess what hardship or privation had caused her to leave the real world for this laughing world of her imagination.

Douglas last saw Denny with a "thundering black eye" which he got in an argument over his dog, Mike, at Athabasca Landing. In spite of his easy-going manner and great enjoyment of life, LaNauze was not a man whose dog could be insulted.

PLATE 70

From Athabasca Landing they reached Edmonton by land, then the CNR carried them home. On the train, Douglas wrote: "We are passing rapidly eastward over the great Canadian plain, sitting in warmth and comfort in a luxurious dining car. No slimy, muddy moccasins are on our feet now, and no caribou hairs on these steaks, but we didn't think the bread any better than our bannock, and the soup is distinctly inferior to that we made at Hodgson's Point."

Outside the train windows, it was snowing heavily. "We are talking of our late companions of the north; of LaNauze and the Indians making their way back to Chipewyan in such weather as this; of Hornby and how winter must have set in with him."

The long journey ended appropriately: Lionel and George paddled up Katchiwano Lake to Northcote Farm, "we are back on clear waters and among woods of unequalled beauty. ... That dear poplar-crested ridge comes in sight; the trees have held their leaves to the last to welcome us, and red against their yellow, the flag proclaims that we are home at last."

PLATE 70

Chapter 10
Northern Attraction

After he reached home in the autumn of 1912, it took some time for Douglas to realize how the North had changed him. Even then he was not sure which changes were in himself, which in the world around him. At the end of *Lands Forlorn* he wrote: "Some time passed before we began to feel in many subtle ways the results of a long absence. ... while we were relatively unaltered our world had gone on its appointed course, and unhastening, unceasing, the appointed changes had been wrought. It was ground irrevocably lost: no skill, nor energy, nor address, could recover it. The times had changed, the change in ourselves had no reference to them but made conformity to established usages more than ever difficult."

Apparently it had occurred to Douglas already that he did not fit well within the fast-changing society of the twentieth century. By inclination he was a loner, a dreamer; in his professional life he was a planner, a leader, an organizer, but never "one of the boys." He was also partially deaf and deafness made it hard to communicate, easier to keep his own counsel.

Lands Forlorn was published in July 1914. A few weeks later the Great War broke out and suddenly everything was changed. Even Hornby was rooted out of the North by the rousing call to war. On September 8 he arrived at Northcote Farm, confused, misplaced, still out-of step with civilization, but bound to enlist for England and the Empire.

That fall the world knew no more idyllic place than Northcote Farm. Its large white house on the hill looked out on three sides toward the water. The early log houses, dating back to 1840, seemed to grow out of the earth itself. Hornby arrived in a place of coloured leaves, of flocking songbirds and waterfowl, and always the sound of water against the shore. Northcote would be a bright memory of tranquillity to carry with him into the trenches of the First World War.

From Hornby, George acquired news of the past winter at Hodgson's Point, not all of it good. He had given Rouvière and LeRoux permission to live in the Douglas house but had given Hornby a note saying that part of the stores there were to be his. It was an awkward situation and quarrelling soon broke out. Moreover, LeRoux turned Arimo away from Hornby and Hornby never forgave him for this. Hornby told scandalous tales about a relationship between Arimo and the priest. His own relationship with her had been blissfully uncomplicated. Losing her was symbolic of losing the perfect peace this land had offered him for a time.

Rouvière had also offended the Englishman by taking Harry to Fort Franklin when he knew Hornby needed him for his trip to the Coppermine. According to Hornby, Rouvière's relations with the Inuit had deteriorated. The priests had a difficult six-week crossing of Great Bear Lake which meant that they arrived late, missing many of the Inuit at Lake Rouvière. Then, in October, Hornby had fallen ill at Lake Rouvière while the father was out at Great Bear getting winter fish. Douglas could see that Father LeRoux must have cared for him and lost valuable good-weather time for seeking souls. Yet Hornby expressed nothing but contempt for him.

In January 1913, Hornby travelled out to Fort Norman with Rouvière. On the way back he decided to stay at Franklin, leaving the priest to make the cold crossing with only a small Indian boy, a journey on which he might easily have perished.

A letter from Captain Joe Bernard on Coronation Gulf reached the priests in August. It urged them to come and set up a mission there. Filled with excitement they started to plan the trip although it was already September. Hornby had had enough. He packed his things and left Dease Bay in September 1913 with some Indian companions in the Douglas York boat, *Jupiter*.

Near Gros Cap he was caught in a storm which wrecked the boat on the shores of what was now called Douglas Bay. All on board survived although he lost most of his furs and collection of artifacts. With what he could salvage, he and the Indians went on by canoe to Franklin. He then spent the winter of 1913-14 at Fort Franklin and Fort Norman, and in travelling down the Mackenzie to the sea.

At Fort Norman Hornby met D'Arcy Arden. Arden was born in Ottawa in 1880 where his father, an army man from Cork, was stationed. He had attended Ridley College and trained for the Royal Navy but was rejected because he was too short. At the age of seventeen or eighteen, he went to Labrador with a government survey party.

Hornby seemed preoccupied and uneasy about this newcomer. He told Douglas about the "college boy's" traumatic initiation to the North. For forty days his Labrador party starved. Most of the men got scurvy and, when food did become available, three men died of overeating. After that D'Arcy tried office work with the Topographical Survey in Ottawa but soon asked to be sent north again. For the next ten years, he was part of the Yukon gold rush. In 1911 he left the Yukon for survey work on Herschel Island. While there he heard tales of Great Bear Lake and of Melville and Hornby, and began to plan a trip across the lake and overland to the Arctic coast where he would set up trade with the Inuit.

Douglas could picture Hornby sizing up Arden at Fort Norman, jealous because he was going into Coppermine country, but attracted by his plans, wondering if he could travel with him and achieve the delicate balance of freedom and human contact he had known on Dease Bay two winters ago. From his repetitious talk about the young man, Douglas knew that a great longing for the Barren Lands had almost made Hornby turn around and travel back. But stronger than the call of the Coppermine in 1914 was a call from outside. As Hornby put it, he answered the "Call of Patriotism."

In spite of his personal bitterness, Hornby's visit had its pleasant times. George showed him some of the Kawartha Lakes and introduced him to the summer crowd of cottage friends.

Hornby, on his way to war, was still undecided how to go about it and seemed to be seeking advice. Douglas advised him to go to England and take a commission. Hornby left Lakefield and did the opposite, joining the Alberta Dragoons in Valcartier, Quebec, as a private.

Shortly after Hornby left, Douglas went to New York to offer himself for enlistment at the British Consulate General. He was turned down because of his partial deafness. In his school days, as the brothers paddled down Katchiwano Lake to Sheldrake's school at Lakefield, they noticed that Lionel could hear the bell when George couldn't. George had never considered his hearing a problem and was upset now at being rejected. He sailed for England in January 1915 and there was rejected again by both the Flying Corps and the Royal Navy.

For Douglas, whose Uncle Archie had been an admiral in the Royal Navy and whose father won the Victoria Cross which lay in a drawer at Northcote Farm, this was indeed a heavy blow.

While Lionel served in the Navy, George was finally appointed to one of the Armstrong armament works as an engineering-supervisor but his service there was short-lived. Practical and efficient American ways of doing things had left him little patience for hide-bound British ways. The plant manager was studying the hub of an 18-pound field gun which was "made of a fancy bronze, at a fancy price," when he asked Douglas for an opinion on it. Douglas said shortly, "Make it of cast steel," a reply that was tantamount to blasphemy. Before long he decided that Armstrong's was not the place for him. He took passage back to America and went to work in Tombstone, Arizona, "with good American engineers" putting abandoned mines back to work to handle the war-time demand for lead, zinc and copper. August Sandberg was there too, working with him to start a modern flotation plant at one of the old mills. In six months, the plant was working well and Douglas came home to Northcote for a year.

In September 1916 he took a job as consultant in a plant in Mexico. The next April he returned to Canada briefly to marry Frances Mackenzie and take her back with him. Frances, the daughter of a mathematics professor at the University of Toronto, was part of a large family which came to Stoney Lake every summer. Her uncle was headmaster of the Grove School (formerly

Sheldrake's School, known today as Lakefield College School). Although twenty years younger than George, it was obvious that she had much in common with him, sharing his love of the rugged Kawartha landscape, his fascination with the world, and his delight in the beauty of simple things.

Not long after the Douglas couple arrived in Mexico, they heard that August Sandberg had been thrown in jail in Phoenix, Arizona. Dr Sandberg had trained in Germany and had worked a great deal with German people. He held a high opinion of their technical ability. In the United States in 1917, anti-German feeling ran very high. Sandberg's nature was more blunt than diplomatic; his touting of German engineering superiority ignored the emotional atmosphere of war-time America. Before long, he was branded a German sympathizer and arrested.

The Douglases raced to Phoenix where they talked to the authorities and rescued their friend from jail. But the incident changed Sandberg's life. His job had been given to someone else and he never went back to engineering. The affair "broke him up" and he went to live with his brother in California.

The Douglases spent most of 1918 in Mexico and came home for Christmas just as the troops were coming home. With them came an epidemic of deadly influenza. Frances felt sick by the time she reached Chicago; by the time she reached Toronto she was dreadfully ill. "I had the flu in Toronto," she recalls. "My husband went on to New York and had it there."

Toronto schools, including the one behind the Mackenzie house where Frances herself lay sick, had been turned into hospitals for returning soldiers who had the flu. She recalls a young friend who had survived the war and was met at Union Station by his eager, thankful parents. They were told that he showed symptoms of the flu and could not go home with them. He was sent instead to the school-hospital behind the Mackenzie house, and died there.

For George and Frances Douglas, Northcote Farm was a perfect haven from the ills of the world. They came home now to convalesce and to assimilate the changes brought by the war. They had much to be grateful for. Lionel had survived his service with the Navy on the Red Sea. He was now stationed on Canada's west coast with the Canadian Pacific's transpacific service.

Douglas discovered that even here in the quiet peace of the Kawartha Lakes, his spirit turned northward. His reading, letter writing, conversations and daydreaming were often focused on northern places and northern people. Nothing pleased him more than a letter or a visit from someone who could talk about Great Bear Lake. Along with the good laughs and warm memories such a preoccupation provided there was sometimes anxiety, dismay and shock.

Bits of news received from other Northerners about John Hornby were disturbing. Hornby survived the war. He had been badly wounded but, as soon as he could travel, he sailed for Canada, apparently without leave. He came to Northcote in the late summer of 1916 only to find Douglas away in Mexico. Not knowing that his mother had sent money for him to an Edmonton bank, he wired Douglas for money. Douglas sent it and Hornby made his way north. But in 1918 a letter to Douglas from D'Arcy Arden described Hornby's condition as pitiable. "He is not fit for this country now."[1]

Another 1918 letter from the North brought shocking news. Father Rouvière had been murdered.[2]

Chapter 11
Denny LaNauze and the Rouvière-Le Roux Murders

The news came in a long letter from Denny LaNauze, the RNWMP corporal who had travelled up-river with Douglas in 1912. Denny was then twenty-five. Three years later he was ordered to embark on one of the most hazardous and seemingly hopeless man-hunts ever undertaken by the scarlet force.

From Hornby's visit in the fall of 1914, Douglas knew that the priests had left the Dease late in the season to travel with the Inuit to the coast. He could picture them without provisions of their own, without proper clothing, dependent on the their native guides, walking directly into the blizzards of the Arctic. Why?

Had Coronation Gulf become an obsession, a goal to be reached regardless of the cost? Were all Rouvière's attempts to Christianize the Inuit failing, was he becoming desperate? Did he believe that by living with them as Stefansson had done, he and LeRoux could achieve perfect understanding of them?

Whatever his thinking, he and LeRoux had turned their faces north into the darkness of the year. They speak to us once more from a diary found by the LaNauze party not far from Bloody

Falls. The last entry dated November 1913 reads: "We are dissatisfied with the Eskimo, we have little to eat, and we do not know what to do."[1]

Douglas could picture them turning south, poorly clad, emotionally defeated, their dogs unfed, without provisions or a plan and possibly angry with each other. Two Inuit, Sinnisiak and Uluksuk, travelled in the same direction.

Two years passed after the disappearance of the priests before LaNauze was sent North.

> I was five months at Regina with a squadron of ours, and got 24 hours notice in May 1915 to go North and look for the Fathers Rouvière and LeRoux who were reported missing.
>
> The party was two men and myself, we outfitted at Edmonton, where I was fortunate enough to obtain a copy of *Lands Forlorn* which proved to be of great value to me later on.

Denny's two men were Constable Withers and Constable Wight. Travelling with the three police were an Oblate priest named Father Frapsauce, an Inuit interpreter, Ilavinik, and D'Arcy Arden.

Arden had precipitated the manhunt. When he came out to Fort Norman in the spring of 1915 and reported that Inuit had been seen wearing cassocks and surplices, the Mounted Police had to act. By this time Arden's knowledge of the Coppermine country was quite extensive and LaNauze realized he could use his help.

LaNauze bought an old York boat at Resolution for $125 and went down past Fort Norman to McPherson to get an Inuit interpreter. "We left Fort Norman on July 15th, 1915. I had about 5 tons of stuff, York boat, 2 canoes, 2 teams of dogs."

The party had a difficult crossing of Great Bear Lake: "nothing but North-Easters."

> It was not until September 15th that we reached the Narrows, where the missing priests had made their base after you left. The place was just about 8 miles from the Dease mouth, on the N.E. shore of Dease Bay, and not where old Fort Confidence stands. It was just 3 miles East of the fishing place in that clump of big spruce. It was a good

spot for our base, for as you know we had to fish, and there was lots of Lion's friends, the 'dry spruce trees.'

We built one storehouse and occupied the priests quarters, and I got a little cabin from Harry for 40 skins for one year.

Mention of Harry brought back to George Douglas a memory of the Indian boy cooking bacon for the first "strangers" met on the Barrens. Harry would be grown-up he supposed, seventeen or eighteen. LaNauze described him as "a biggish young man now, and quite capable."

Once his winter quarters were established on Dease Bay the corporal knew he had little time to lose if he hoped to reach the priests' other cabin on Lake Rouvière before the winter storms set in. "Harry took us out to Lake Rouvière, we walked and packed as the Dease was frozen by early September."

In late September they found the cabin in the small clump of dry spruce at the extreme northeast end of the lake. "It was in ruins, half burnt down, *not a clue of any kind* to show the whereabouts or probably destination of the missing priests."

They had come to a dead end in their search, a blackened burned-out cabin surrounded by thousands of square miles of white frozen tundra. They had trekked across Lake Rouviere toward the clump of spruce, toward a vision of four stout walls, a stove and the comfort of a night indoors. Now the cold pierced their parkas as they stood there desolate.

With the season so far advanced, LaNauze had no choice but to turn back to winter quarters. The disappointment and the rigors of the long trail back were lightened by their good luck in finding caribou, a herd of 400 travelling north-west. He and Ilavinik killed 25 and then added two moose to their larder near Observation Hill. The long winter ahead looked better with that meat in cache. In a heavy snowstorm they reached their base on Great Bear again on October 4 after a 180-mile trek.

The winter of 1915-16 swirled around them in the cabin on the north-east shore of Bear Lake. It was a "good winter." LaNauze gave Douglas news of Harry, Modeste and the other Bear Lakers and reported on the Douglas cabin at Hodgson's Point:

Hodgson's Point was still intact when we left, but regarding your stuff there is mighty little left, as after the priests were murdered some of the Eskimos came inland the next summer and pillaged everything in sight. We even found altar cloths in Coronation Gulf. All the priest stuff was also stolen, some of the stuff being seen by the CAE's at Bathurst Inlet. Regarding the theft of property, all I could do was to warn the Eskimos that it would not be tolerated in future. They produced a lot of stuff, some I presume of yours, and wanted to give it back to me, but I was not in a position to carry it.

In January some of the Indians went over the ice for mail and Father Frapsauce, " ... the most ideal character I have ever met ...," left them to return to Fort Norman. Meanwhile LaNauze made his plans for spring:

I had decided that if any trace was to be found of the priests it would be on the Arctic Coast, as the Indians knew nothing, except Harry and his mother 'Aranmore' [Arimo], who had seen Father Rouvière in September 1913, and he was then leaving Dease Bay to pick up Father LeRoux, and accompany the Eskimos to the coast, and would be away possibly for two years. It was up to us to reach the coast before the Eskimos left the sea ice.

On March 29th we left Dease Bay, and struck the mouth of the Coppermine a month later. At the mouth of the Coppermine we found fresh sled tracks, and followed them East for 35 miles, and fell in with a travelling party of the Canadian Arctic Expedition. Accompanying them was Corporal Bruce of the Herschel Island detachment, who had been sent in with the Expedition the previous summer by sea to work on the case. No news had been gained of the priests.

We then struck west across Coronation Gulf, and about a week later, in a little snow hut off Cape Lambert, in the Dolphin and Union Straits, the whole mystery came out. There we learnt that the unfortunate missionaries had been cruelly murdered by two Copper Eskimos. The act was greatly deplored by the tribe, and after we once got a line on the case we had no difficulty in obtaining the information. We got some supplies from the Canadian Arctic Expedition base near Port Cockbourne in the Straits, and then struck out after the murderers.

On May 15th the principal murderer 'Sinnisiak' was arrested on the South Coast of Victoria Land, and a week later the second, 'Uluksuk,' was arrested on an island opposite the mouth of the Coppermine, about eight miles out to sea.

LaNauze added "There is nothing that would give me greater pleasure than to meet Lion and yourself, and have a real good talk about that country. I only hope I will be able to some day." That day came in the summer of 1928 when he came to visit at Northcote Farm. In conversations in the big white house and on the shores of Katchiwano, Denny filled in some of the details of his Arctic trek -- the bad April blizzard and the ravine near the Dismal Lakes that gave them shelter, their first view of the Coppermine River on Easter Sunday, the warm welcome at an Inuit village when they reached the coast at 5 p.m. on April 30 after a month of travel.

I sure was pleased to find Corporal Bruce of the Herschel Island detachment travelling with Mr Chipman's Arctic Expedition with instructions to connect with my patrol. On the 3rd of May we had a blizzard, a bad blizzard ... we could not stand up in it. When that was over Arden left us to go east with Chipman and Corporal Bruce joined my party acting as guide.

They headed west, questioning people in villages along the way. Finally, near Cape Lambert they met a man named Nachim:

We saw that someone knew something here. Ilavinik suggested that we go to Nachim's house, and we were escorted to a small snow hut in the middle of the village. There, in this faraway spot on the Arctic coast, the mystery of the missing priests was revealed to us.

I sat back and let Ilavinik do the talking. I stayed perfectly still and in about five minutes Ilavinik said to me, 'I got him. The priests were killed by Husky, all right;

these men very, very sorry.' The two men had covered their faces with their hands and there was dead silence in the igloo.

An Eskimo named Koeha did most of the talking. He spoke of the white men staying in a tent with one named Kormik. Kormik took the priests' rifle and LeRoux got angry. Then Kormik was angry and wanted to kill him. Koeha then helped the priests to get away. He held Kormik and then told Kormik's mother to hold him while he helped the priests to pack their sled. Koeha told me that he and another Eskimo each gave the priests a dog and they had two of their own. Then Koeha went up the river with them pulling the sled in the harness as far as he could see his own tents. Then he shook hands with the Fathers. When he last saw them, Ilogoak (LeRoux) was running ahead of the sled and Kuleavik (Rouvière) was driving the sled. The sun was already very low.

Koeha then told how two men named Uluksak and Sinnisiak left to go up-river two nights later. When they came back, Uluksak told how he and Sinnisiak had killed the two priests.

Douglas and Denny spread out a map and traced the route that LaNauze took north-west on the trail of Sinnisiak. The clues led to the Liston and Sutton Islands and then to the coast of Victoria Land where they came upon a cluster of skin tents.

Our guide took us to a canvas tent. In it a man sat making a bow. He appeared to be stunned with fear, and I learnt afterward that he expected to be stabbed immediately. I explained that he had to come with us and finally the other Eskimos, grasping the situation, convinced him that he must go.

We took Sinnisiak back to Bernard Harbour and then set out to the mouth of the Coppermine where we heard Uluksak might now be found. We found him on one of the islands and he ran forward holding up his hands.

My problem now was to get the prisoners back to civilization. I judged it best to take them out via Herschel Island. The truth was I thought I might lose them if we went overland to Great Bear Lake in the company of other Eskimos. Their old dread of Indians surfaced too and they wanted to know if I had to take them into Indian country. So I left Constables Wight and Ilavinik at the mouth of the Coppermine to visit the scene of the murder and go out by Bear Lake while Corporal Bruce and I took the prisoners back to Bernard Harbour to travel on the *Alaska* to Herschel Island. We wintered there and I brought them up the Mackenzie in the following spring.

Douglas had followed the Calgary trial of the two murderers as it was reported in the newspapers and knew some of the details. The two accused gave statements which were straightforward, gruesome but at the same time, strangely innocent. It was easy to picture the desperate scene on the Coppermine, LeRoux meeting the two Inuit on the trail, forcing them to pull the sleds south, away from their homes into a land where Inuit never went in winter. Their panic is graphic in the words of Sinnisiak:

> I was thinking hard and crying and very scared and the frost was in my boots and I was cold. I wanted to go back, but I was afraid. Ilogoak would not let us. Every time the sled stuck, Ilogoak would pull out the rifle. I got hot inside my body and every time Ilogoak pulled out the rifle I was very much afraid.
>
> I said to Uluksak, 'I think they will kill us.' I can't get back now, I was thinking, I will not see my people anymore; I will try and kill him. I was pulling ahead of the dogs. We came to a small hill. I took off the harness quick and ran to one side and Ilogoak ran after me and pushed me back to the sled. I took off my belt and told Ilogoak I was going to relieve myself, as I did not want to go to the sled. After that I ran behind the sled, I did not want to relieve myself. Then Ilogoak turned round and saw me, he looked away from me and I stabbed him in the back with a knife.

"That first day of their trial," LaNauze recalled, "was a hot day. They appeared in skin clothing with their feet in tubs of ice water, an attempt by the defence to show the jury the enormous cultural gap they were dealing with here."

Douglas understood that gap. He questioned LaNauze about the people he met, the camps on the Coppermine and the Arctic coast in the spring of 1916. LaNauze told of the camp at Bernard Harbour where sealing operations were finishing for the season. Most of the Inuit were already moving inland to fish and hunt deer. Over 100 were gathered at the mouth of the Coppermine. "Isn't it hard to realize that these people were an unknown race before 1910 living a stone age existence. For fire they had iron pyrites and tinder, seal blubber for fuel, bows and spears for hunting and skins for clothing. They had soapstone for cooking pots and lamps, native copper for their weapons."

"What did you think of them as people?"

Denny gave them his highest praise: "They were kind to their children and good to their dogs."

Sinnisiak and Uluksuk were found guilty of murder and sentenced to death, the sentence commuted almost at once to imprisonment for life. In 1919 they were pardoned and sent home to Coppermine country.

Chapter 12
Northern Connections

When he left the North in 1912, Douglas believed that nothing could prevent his return. In fact he did not return for sixteen years. In 1914 the Great War broke out. Then in 1918 James Douglas, whose interest in the copper bearing possibilities of Great Bear might have sent him back, died. Douglas knew of the oil strike near Fort Norman and the resulting parade of prospectors down the Mackenzie, but his own work in Mexico and Arizona provided no opportunity for a trip north.

In spite of these obstacles to his return, Douglas remained attentive to events in the north and his northern connections strengthened with the passing years. He became a Fellow of the American Geographical Society, the American Association for the Advancement of Science and the Arctic Institute of North America. He belonged to the American Society of Mechanical Engineers, the Canadian Institute of Mining and Metallurgy and the American Institute of Mining and Metallurgical Engineers. He wrote articles for the *Canadian Mining and Metallurgical Bulletin and for the Engineering and Mining Journal Press*. He became a member of the Arts and Letters Club of Toronto and the Explorers Club in New York.

Douglas regularly wrote to friends and acquaintances in the North. His best correspondent from Great Bear Lake was D'Arcy Arden. Douglas first wrote to him in 1918 after hearing a great deal about him from Hornby and LaNauze. LaNauze, in describing his trek after the priests' murderers, said, "Arden is still in that country, and living with Harry, he is a nice chap, and a capable traveller, but has gone a little 'Bush Crazy', i.e. the country has 'got him.'" Douglas wrote asking Arden for news of Great Bear, of Dease Bay in particular, and of Hornby, François, Harry and old Tow-wy-ee. He wrote of his dream to come back there some day, of "peculiarly vivid longings" for the country between Dease Bay and the Coppermine.

Arden wrote a brief reply on July 31 from Fort Norman before the boat left with the mail, then a longer, newsy letter from his Dease Bay cabin on December 1. "I often come across your trails," he wrote, "and I often think how I would like to show [you] some of this country you did not see." [1]

By this time Arden had established a good trading business and had begun a fox ranch as well. His fur trade was mainly with the Inuit at Dismal Lakes where Harry, who now spoke Inuit as well as English and his native Loucheaux, was stationed. Hornby had moved away from Dease Bay to Hornby Bay.

The Inuit also had changed from the "strangers" Douglas saw nine years earlier. They stayed inland longer, dressed in Western Inuit or white-man style; used rifles, tents and stoves; and were fond of white man's grub: "... I very much regret to say they are not as well off now as before. I have a poor boy here now dying of consumption caused simply by changing from skin clothing into White man's clothing."

The Oblate mission continued to be plagued by misfortune. Father Frapsauce had travelled with Arden and LaNauze as far as Rouvière's house in the 1915 search: "...well the poor fellow was starting another mission to the Eskimo here, and was drowned last Oct. He went through the thin ice with his Sled & Dogs all were lost and we have not as yet found any trace of them. The mission to the Eskimos seem to have hard luck indeed. Don't they?" [2]

Although his letters to Arden were motivated primarily by a need for news of northern friends, they were probably "good business" as well. Douglas kept a close eye on northern discovery and development and by 1920 Arden's fortunes were becoming tied to oil and mineral exploration. When oil was struck near Fort Norman that year he sold Imperial Oil some land below Bear Rock for $2000. A year later he wrote to Douglas about his prospects:

> I am far more interested in finding placers in some of these Cambrian sediments in McTavish Bay and back of Big Stick Island. I have a notion that some of these sediments contain gold. I have a very good man working now, one of the discoverers of the Klondyke, Tom Kirkpatrick by name, you may have heard of him. There is very good looking black sand in some of the creeks, and an awful lot of copper.[3]

Arden also kept Douglas posted on the vicissitudes of Hornby's life. No friendship was possible between the two men. Arden had scrapped his plan to live on the coast and settled down on Dease Bay, the country which Hornby in his heart claimed as his own. Not only did Arden have the allegiance and trade of all the Indians and Inuit in the Coppermine country, he also had Arimo. Hornby found the situation intolerable and went on to Caribou Bay (already being called Hornby Bay) a small inlet within the large sweep of Hunter's Bay on the southeast corner of Great Bear Lake.

In 1917 he began a bad winter by cutting himself with an axe. All fall he had to crawl. Since he depended on fishing to live and his nets were three miles from his house, and since he had to make the trip four times a week with temperatures often down to 70° below zero, his survival that winter was a miracle. At times the Indians must have helped him. But in March 1918, Arden went to see him and found him, "...starving and completely out of his head." Later that winter he brought Hornby to Dease Bay, probably saving his life.

Hornby's own letters were sporadic but, with these and scraps of information from other northern acquaintances, Douglas was able to keep track of his erratic travels.

In June 1919, he left Great Bear Lake and went out to Edmonton. Thinking that the frozen paradise that eluded him at the east end of Great Bear Lake might be found at the east end of Great Slave Lake, he headed north again in the late summer of 1919 only to be frozen in and forced to winter at Chipewyan. In the spring of 1920 he was off again. He now aimed to reach Artillery Lake, but he was unable to get an outfit together and found himself again stuck near Reliance.

He almost starved during the winter of 1920-21 and limped back to Resolution in June. Because Douglas had hinted that he might be interested in exploring on Great Slave Lake, Hornby wrote urging him to come. He felt that Douglas could "set things straight" for him. He was also thinking of writing a book which he wanted Douglas to edit. Its title was to be *Land of Feast or Famine.*

"I have certainly spent a life-time & unless I publish a successful book, I must admit it to have been a rather fruitless & at the same time a damn lonesome existence."[4]

Douglas heard nothing more of Hornby until the spring of 1922 when Guy Blanchet, heading east to begin his survey of the eastern end of Great Slave Lake for the Topographical Survey of Canada, discovered Hornby, all skin-and-bones heading by canoe out to Resolution. "We picked up Hornby who said he had been held up for days by the ice and was starving."[5]

Blanchet found in Hornby a pilot who knew the intricacies of the eastern end of Great Slave Lake with uncanny accuracy. Hornby informed Blanchet that the bay south of Preble Point was actually a channel because Preble Point was actually an island. This was news to both Blanchet and his Indian pilot, the famed Sousie Beaulieu, but they took Hornby's word for it and he guided them through. He then sat down and drew Blanchet a "remarkably good" map of the eastern arm of Great Slave Lake. In return for his help, Hornby feasted on Blanchet's rations and "made frequent trips down below to make tea."[5]

Hornby made his way out to Edmonton with the idea of returning to England. He wrote that he wanted to visit Northcote Farm on the way but Douglas was in the southern states. Hornby changed plans and took a job guiding American hunters in the Rockies.

From 1922 to 1924 he seemed to be attempting to organize and regularize his life but confusion and uncertainty still dogged his efforts. He wrote Douglas about photos for the book he was planning to write. He met an English adventurer named James Charles Critchell-Bullock and began to plan an expedition with him to Artillery Lake. He also befriended Olwen Newell, a girl twenty years younger than himself. In March 1924 he visited Ottawa to talk to Dr R.M.

Anderson about funds for a three-year scientific expedition. He then went on to England to visit his ailing parents.

While in England he met Guy Blanchet again. Blanchet offered him a position on a surveying party which was going into Artillery and Mackay Lakes. Why Hornby did not accept is a mystery. On the survey, his unique knowledge of the terrain and his wilderness skills could have been organized and put to use. On his own, he allowed his talents to go off in all directions and could not even manage to feed himself consistently.

In June 1924, he returned to Canada and came to Northcote. Douglas wrote to LaNauze that he found Hornby incoherent about his recent whereabouts and about his future plans.

Douglas next heard that Guy Blanchet met Hornby with Bullock and a few other trappers at Reliance, all heading into the Barrens to winter. Blanchet gave them a lift in the *Ptarmigan* to the beginning of Pike's Portage.

What followed was a winter miserable and strange even by Hornby standards. He and Bullock dug a habitation in the side of an esker and in this crude cave they spent the winter. Bullock found Hornby's eating and living habits insupportably dirty. The tension in the cave was electric.

In May Hornby and Bullock headed out with an impressive winter's catch of furs – not west but east. Hornby had already begun to dream of the Thelon River as his elusive place of perfection, and was determined to see it now. At the end of July he stood and gazed at the oasis of timber just below the junction of the Hanbury with the Thelon. He would come back to this place as soon as he could.

Again, starvation stalked them and they were in bad shape before they reached the post at Baker Lake. From there they traveled to Chesterfield Inlet and took their furs by ship to St. John's, Newfoundland, only to find that in their damp cave the furs had not cured properly and were worthless. In good condition those furs might have brought the two men $14,000.

Yet that crazy winter in the cave produced the one lasting achievement of Hornby's life. He had been commissioned by the federal government to write a report on caribou. He went to Ottawa promptly from St. John's and did so. The result was the establishment of the 15,000 square mile Thelon Game Sanctuary for the protection of Barren Land wildlife, musk-ox in particular.

Meanwhile D'Arcy Arden's fortunes also changed. When he wrote to Douglas in November 1924, he had moved to Fort Smith. Now his letters mirrored the same peculiar longing for the Coppermine that Douglas expressed.

The whole south shore of Great Bear Lake from the head of the Bear to the mouth of the Dease had been made an Indian reserve. Arden had been moved out of this paradise and given a post as warden of Wood Buffalo Park near Fort Smith.

"I sold my place to the Hudsons Bay Co. I can assure you I was very sorry to part with it. I had a lovely place there ... I can assure you I am more than anxious to get back to the so-called Barren Grounds."[6]

Meanwhile Hornby turned in his caribou report and returned again to England; he was there when his father died. He arrived back in Canada in 1926 with Edgar Christian, the 17-year-old son of his favourite cousin, Marguerite (Hornby) Christian. In Ottawa they saw Guy Blanchet who tried to dissuade the boy from going north with Hornby. But Christian had adopted his mother's admiration for her cousin. Hornby had become his hero.

As usual Hornby wrote Douglas in the hope he might be planning a trip north but Douglas was in Arizona again. Instead the two Englishmen visited Mrs Douglas and her father, Professor Michael Mackenzie, in Toronto before heading west:

> After dinner we sat around in my father's study. Hornby told us he was going north-east of Great Slave Lake. Dad asked him about the preparations he was making and Hornby said he didn't need any: 'I know the land well. I can live off the land the way the Indians do.'
>
> Dad said, 'But occasionally the Indians starve.'
>
> That remark didn't make any impression on either Hornby or young Christian who was lost in hero-worship of Hornby. The poor lad was bewitched.
>
> When we saw them off at the station, Edgar showed more competence than his uncle.

Hornby thought they had missed their train but Edgar figured out the change from Daylight Saving Time to railroad time correctly. Edgar had the tickets and was in charge of all the luggage.

We watched them go with a strong feeling that this was a dangerous expedition for the boy. My father was very much upset.[7]

Mrs Douglas always believed that George was the one person who might have convinced Hornby not to take Edgar along. Blanchet and friends had tried and failed in Ottawa; now she and her father had failed in Toronto.

In Winnipeg Hornby saw Olwen Newell and proposed to her. Olwen declined. On May 11, on the train speeding west from Winnipeg, Hornby wrote to George Douglas:

I was very sorry not to have seen you at Toronto & regret that you can not go North this year. I am heartily sick of the North & I wish I had never buried myself in the wilds. In all probability, I shall only make a trip to bring out a few more samples & then perhaps may settle down somewhere on Vancouver Island. Will write again, when I reach Edmonton.[8]

Douglas heard nothing further.

When Denny LaNauze arrived at Northcote Farm for a visit in the late winter of 1928 their conversation about George's plan to go north in the spring was shadowed by uneasiness about the Hornby party. The previous November Douglas had written to Inspector Trundle of the Royal Canadian Mounted Police at Fort Smith:

I want to get in touch with Hornby as I expect to make a trip into the Slave Lake country next summer, and would like to know as soon as possible if he would care to join my party at Fort Smith or Fort Resolution in June.

If you happen to see him on your patrol, or if you are able to get word to him, will you please let him know my intentions and tell him to write or wire to me at Lakefield, Ontario. Any news of interest about him please wire to me collect at Lakefield Ontario on your return.

Hornby may have come out by Hudson's Bay again, and I'll write to your head-quarters at Ottawa in case they know anything about him through their Chesterfield Inlet Post. ...[9]

In December the *New York Times* ran a piece from Ottawa saying that officials there were concerned about the fate of John Hornby. Stefansson saw this and wrote a worried letter to O.S. Finnie, Director of the Northwest Territories and Yukon Branch of the Department of the Interior. Finnie replied that a scientific party going to the Thelon Game Sanctuary the next summer would look for Hornby.

In January Douglas sent letters to both Fort Smith and Resolution addressed to Hornby:

Nothing has been heard of you for so long that we are feeling much anxiety about you. I was in Ottawa about a month ago, and saw our various friends there. I hope all is well.

I am planning a trip into Slave Lake this summer, and should certainly like you to join the party. Of course you would be remunerated for your services, and if you know of any minerals that would be of interest it is a good chance to bring them to notice and secure your interests.

I am keeping 'space' and supplies for you anyway. If this comes to you please let me know by telegram from Smith, collect how you are, and whether I can depend on you for next summer....[10]

As time passed there were reports of Hornby sighted here and heard of there. LaNauze assured Douglas that the RCMP would check these as best they could. In late winter the force ran a Hudson Bay patrol out of Chesterfield Inlet along the coast from Cambridge Bay to Bernard Harbour because of a 'sighting' there, and Inspector Trundle questioned everyone he could find at Reliance. Douglas planned his spring trip with space and supplies for Hornby.

PLATE 71

In the spring of 1928 Douglas at last had his chance to go North again. United Verde of Clarkedale, Arizona, financed his exploration for copper on the isolated, uninhabited and unexplored south-east shore of Great Slave Lake. He planned a trip that would cover in detail 600 miles of convoluted coastline, the first extensive geological investigation ever made of the area.

> It was partly Blanchet's reports, partly because the area had been described in places as 'Keweenawan,' partly that I had seen samples of high-grade copper ore brought out by Hornby from somewhere in that country, and finally the lack of definite knowledge about an area so important, that led me to advise exploration thereof as a venture that might be rewarded.[1]

In Edmonton Douglas picked up the company's field geologist, Carl Lausen. They left Edmonton on May 22. Where Douglas had travelled by stage and canoe and sweated with the Athabasca Brigade in 1911, they could now bypass the 200 miles of rapids and go as far as Waterways near McMurray by rail. Later he wrote, "... I don't think I ever saw anything even in Mexico quite as bad as the railroad between Edmonton and WW."[2]

PLATE 72

After the 1920 strike by Imperial Oil 82 km (51 miles) north of Fort Norman, explorers, prospectors, geologists and fortune-seekers began pouring down the Mackenzie system.

In Ottawa the federal government perked up its ears. Although The Northwest Territories Act in 1905 made provision for a self-governing council, in actual fact a small group of civil servants working in several government agencies handled northern affairs. They did very little. Phrases like absent-minded unconcern and benign neglect are used to describe Ottawa's attitude to the North in the early years of the twentieth century.

Two events could cause sudden government interest: a threat to Canada's sovereignty or the discovery of minerals. During the Klondike gold rush, the influx of American prospectors led directly to fears of foreign annexation. Now, as the discovery of oil on the Mackenzie River re-awakened those fears, the government set up the Northwest Territories and Yukon Branch of the Department of the Interior. Programmes were set up to gather information, set up game reserves and enforce laws. The RCMP presence was strengthened. In 1921 a treaty was signed with the Mackenzie Valley Indians guaranteeing hunting rights; providing schools, hospitals, and aid to the elderly; and promising yearly payments in exchange for the take-over of their lands. Yet most of the humanitarian work in the North continued to be done by non-government bodies, the Anglican and Catholic church missions and the trading companies.

As Douglas travelled down the Mackenzie the sense of excitement was almost tangible as men hurried to find and stake oil, coal and mineral sites. At Fitzgerald he photographed army planes engaged in topographic survey work for Northern Aerial Minerals Exploration Limited. The discovery that maps drawn from overlapping photos taken from the air could reveal areas of mineral interest dramatically changed the mode of prospecting in the North.

There was money available for exploration and a mood of optimism to go with it. There was a feeling that the gold, silver and copper known to exist in this vast northland were about to be exploited. No-one knew that the world teetered on the brink of the Great Depression.

PLATE 72

PLATE 73

Douglas decided to pass up the HBC transportation and travel north from Waterways by canoe and outboard motor, "... a good preliminary breaking in for Carl," who had scarcely been in a canoe before.

"Our journey down the river was really very pleasant and gave us a good chance to see life at the posts."[3] For Lausen, but especially for himself, this was a taste of the old North: moving leisurely down the rivers and expecting to wait a week for your freight when you arrived, where time was measured in weeks, months, years, never in days.

But on the portage between Fitzgerald and Fort Smith there was evidence of the new, faster pace of life for both white and Inuit. The Ryan brothers, Mickey and Pat, had built a new road: Douglas photographed a four-horse team hauling the *Sea Queen* over the portage. Inuit in Aklavik had bought her for Arctic fishing.

PLATE 73

PLATE 74

Douglas and Lausen reached Resolution on Great Slave by June 1 to find the lake solidly frozen. On June 22 they were able to move out with 1700 pounds of gear in two canoes, to make their 600-mile reconnaissance of the south-east shore of Great Slave Lake.

The Peterborough canoe, named *Mizar,* was bigger than the 1911 *Aldebaran* and was fitted with a 3 horse-power motor. It was cedar-ribbed and canvas-covered, 20′ long with 54″ beam and 21″ deep. By 1928 the Peterborough Canoe Company had the reputation of making the best canoes in the world. The smaller *Alcor* was a butternut canoe built even closer to home by the Lakefield Canoe Company. It gave Douglas great pleasure to go North with the best of all possible canoes built by men he knew as friends and neighbours.

PLATE 75

From 1921 to 1926, as part of the government's new interest in the North, Guy Blanchet had carried out a "control survey" for the Topographical Branch of the Department of the Interior. Blanchet's reports, Hornby's stories of Great Slave Lake, the high-grade copper ore which Hornby had shown him at Northcote, and the fact that such a large area was unknown, intrigued Douglas. "Until our reconnaissance of 1928, the geology of the country was as vague as its topography had been until Blanchet made his map."[4]

> ... Little or nothing is known about this country, and I was astonished at its roughness.[5]
> ... The extreme eastern end of the lake, especially the double peninsula of the Kaochelli, with Wildbread Bay between, is a strange and bizarre country, full of contradictions and surprises, the latter mostly unpleasant.[6]

Glaciers had gouged the land into ridges and cliffs with muskeg valleys or swamps of thick stunted spruce which almost defied passage. The Snowdrift River which they explored reminded Douglas of the Dease. But the blackflies were far worse than anything experienced on Great Bear. The two men made an arduous, fly-crazed, ten-day trip south-east from the end of Great Slave through a chain of small lakes doing some "...gosh-awful walking and climbing."

PLATE 74

PLATE 75

PLATE 76

July 1928 was hot and dry on Great Slave. Bush fires raged unpleasantly close to the area of exploration.

By early August they were camped at Pekanatui Narrows. On August 4 they made a long trip to the south in the *Alcor* carrying about three gallons of gas and enough tea, sugar and hard tack to last two days if necessary. They were sailing back that night with thunderstorms around them when they saw a fresh column of smoke shoot up in the direction of their camp.

When they reached the site they could see the *Mizar* still intact but their camp was a smouldering ruin. Out of the remains of his tent, Douglas plucked the half-burned handbag containing his papers, records, books, instruments and cash. He and Lausen put out the fire which was creeping close to the gas cans and the canoe. Their campfire on a bare gravelly spot was still wet and could not have been the cause of the fire. Lightning may have struck a tall spruce. Whatever the cause, the whole island was now ablaze and the mainland was also beginning to burn. Hurriedly they gathered up the few charred fragments of tent and bedding, loaded them in the *Mizar* and fled the fire.

> We ran some twelve miles that evening before we were clear of fire and smoke, and camped at a safe and sheltered place. Now we were clear of the accursed fire we could check over our things and estimate our loss, which was serious enough, and which had quite a stunning effect on us. ... To make matters worse the long hot and dry spell had broken in rain, high winds and cold, so that we had lost tent and blankets just at the time when we needed them worst. We had a late tea that night, standing before the fire in a downpour of rain.

The forest fire had cooked supper for them: "I had left a hash made of corned beef and desiccated potatoes all ready to cook, in a tin pail; and all ready and perfectly *cooked* I found it."[7]

Aboard the *Mizar* they had plenty of food, a pack of Lausen's clothes as well as some burlap and tar paper and a small tent they could erect over the central section. In it they sat sewing together the charred fragments of blankets until they had a piece 6 feet long by 3 feet wide.

PLATE 76

PLATE 77

PLATE 77

The next day they huddled under their rags and tatters attempting to keep warm as the storm blew around them. On the 6th they set out in fog and reached another sheltered bay. Here began nine more miserable days of waiting.

> One of the worst days for indecision was August 11th ... The delay, uncertainty and indecision is telling on me. Nearly decided to start at 8:00 a.m., and again at 9:30 a.m. but each time the sky turned more threatening than ever. The barometer was low and fell .1" to 28.7. Big bellying clouds moving slowly SW to NW, some glints of pale sunshine, the air very damp. All signs are for more storm ...

By now Lausen had built himself a shelter in a rock gully using a cover which had been on the *Mizar*. Douglas remained in the boat. "My condition when it rained was not a happy one, and it rained only too often. Fire wood was becoming scarce, and I had my choice of foraging afar for wood, or crawling aboard the cold damp *Mizar* and sitting huddled in tarred wrapping paper, reading a book of which only the upper halves of the pages remained."[8]

On the tenth day after the fire they were able to get underway. They had extremely rough weather all the way back to Resolution.

PLATE 78

From Resolution they travelled on the *Speed* as far as Fort Smith, then took the HBC steamer the rest of the way. The *Speed* was a 35-foot Northern Traders boat with 8-foot beam and powered by a 35 horsepower engine. It was operated by Murphy Services and skippered by Vic Ingraham. "14 of us slept in here and two of us at least wished we were back on the *Mizar*."

PLATE 78

PLATE 79

Hornby at Northcote Farm in 1924.

Douglas came back from his summer's work with no exciting find of copper or other precious metal. Nor did he come upon any sign of Hornby's party.

He came across various rumours and speculations, particularly at Fort Smith, RCMP head-quarters for the area. After the patrol from Chesterfield Inlet had searched along the coast, Inspector Trundle had made a trip to Reliance and questioned any trappers he could find. A new RCMP post was set up at Reliance and Corporal Williams there had instructions to question all trappers as they came in.

Pieces of news were put together. The Stewart brothers, old friends of Hornby, had met him travelling with his young cousin and another young man, Harold Adlard, near Reliance. The Stewarts turned back to have a visit with him. Malcolm Stewart, not liking the look of his supplies, offered to pay for more at the post, and said that Hornby took all the tea, sugar and flour that his canoe would carry. The Northern Traders manager at Reliance said Hornby in-tended to winter near the junction of the Hanbury and Thelon. Two other trappers, Al Greathouse and Gene Olsen, told how they had found a note under a cairn on the Casba River addressed to the Stewarts. The note said that the Hornby party was travelling slowly, had shot a caribou and that the flies were bad.

So Hornby had been travelling slowly! Surely he knew he had to reach the oasis on the Thelon before the September migration of caribou passed through.

PLATE 79

Chapter 14
Haunted by Hornby

In the summer of 1928 while Douglas looked for Hornby along the shores of Great Slave Lake, prospector H.S. Wilson, leading a party of four, decided to travel by the Thelon River to Baker Lake and Chesterfield Inlet. They set out from Resolution just after Douglas.

On July 21 they discovered a cabin on the north bank of the Thelon about 40 miles beyond the Hanbury junction. They landed and found the bodies of three men. By August 7 they had brought the news out to the RCMP at Chesterfield Inlet who telegraphed it to Commissioner Starnes in Ottawa.

Douglas did not hear the news until he returned home to Lakefield that fall. He immediately wrote to Wilson for the facts and a long letter, written November 9, arrived to tell the story.

We discovered the cabin on July 21st, our attention first being attracted to it by signs of fairly recent cutting.

Outside the cabin, lying to one side of the door, and parallel to the front of the cabin, there were two bodies. One body, apparently that of the first man to die, was well wrapped up in burlap with an outer wrapping of canvas, but the second body was rather loosely tied up in a red Hudson Bay blanket. The remains of the third member of the party were found on a bunk in one corner of the cabin and completely covered by a couple of blankets.

... we were unable to find a diary recording the experiences of the party prior to their death.[1]

Another year passed before the RCMP reached the site and found Edgar Christian's journal. The eighteen-year-old boy, dying of starvation, left alone for almost a month, still had enough presence of mind to realize that only the stove could provide safe-keeping for his diary. He let the fire die out, put the diary and letters home under the ashes, and put a piece of paper on top of the stove. The writing was partly gone but, " ... WHO .... LOOK IN STOVE ..." could be made out.

The diary found there has become a classic record of suffering and courage comparable to Scott's Antarctic diary.

Hornby, Christian and Adlard suffered dreadfully through the winter of 1926-27. Jack Hornby died on April 16. He had starved himself in an effort to save the two young men for whose plight he was responsible. In a heart-broken farewell note to Christian's mother, he wrote:

April 11th 1927. I am now laid up in bed, writing this note, which may be perhaps the last from me. Poor Edgar is sitting beside.

We have suffered terrible & awful hardships. Poor Edgar needs a long rest. He has been a perfect companion. He is made of sound material & brought up by a perfect Mother. I trust he returns safely

Yrs V. Affect.
Cousin Jack.[2]

Harold Adlard died on May 4; Christian struggled on alone until June 1st. In his last letter to his mother he wrote:

> Please Don't Blame Dear Jack. He Loves you & me only In this world & tell no one else this but keep it & believe.[3]

How much Hornby's love for Marguerite Christian, his cousin, had to do with his erratic and aimless way of life, is one more facet of Hornby's character open to conjecture. Edgar's devotion to him never wavered. Hornby remained his hero, a man worthy of the ultimate sacrifice.

The rest of the world was not so willing to forgive. Many condemned Hornby for assuming the caribou would come when he, of all white men, should have known better. In his *Caribou Notes* prepared for the government, he had written, "In their migrations and whilst they are roaming around Caribou do not always pass the same localities. ... There are many reasons which cause to deflect and alter the course of the Caribou."[4]

D'Arcy Arden wrote to Douglas: "It is very sad to see him go like that, he was a wonderful traveller and had wonderful powers of endurance ..."[5] But later in an interview in Yellowknife, Arden summed up Hornby in blunter style:

> He was a stubborn man. That's why he's dead.
>
> I said, 'You go there where there are no Indians, Jack, and you'll die. Every time you've starved, Jack, an Indian has come to your assistance. You get away from those Indians, and you'll die like a rat.' ...
>
> When a man doesn't take your advice and he's dead and I'm not, who is right?[6]

Bullock, who spent such a miserable winter with Hornby that other trappers feared they might kill one another, wrote:

> Hornby was a man for whom I had the greatest respect and affection, particularly as on our last trip we almost came to an untimely end on several occasions and conse-

quently were brought together as rarely two men are brought together in this day of artificiality.[7]

Douglas would be haunted by Hornby all his life, Hornby as he "really was" and Hornby the legend. In 1955 he vented his irritation at the world's continued interest in a man who did nothing well and committed the final incompetence of killing two young people along with himself:

> So long as Hornby was alive we were not obliged to think of him. This happy immunity ceased with his inevitable end by starvation and every once in a while for the last 30 years I am under the necessity of writing long letters describing just what he really was in contradiction of what he was supposed to be.[8]

But the early death of Hornby left Douglas and his northern friends with questions that could not be answered. Was Hornby, after all, the one man among northern white men who best understood the Barrens? Every other traveller there – prospector, trader, trapper, geologist, surveyor, bush flyer – contributed to changing the way of life in the North and then decried the changes. Jack Hornby did not do this. He was neither prospector, trader, trapper, nor scientist although he followed a little of all of these pursuits in his haphazard efforts to stay alive. If he had a philosophy it was to live or die as part of the land. To live in the Barrens was the most exhilarating experience he ever encountered. To die there was as natural and acceptable for him as to live there. His crime was to take Christian and Adlard with him into that final loneliness. He died tragically aware of that awful mistake.

PLATE 80

In 1932 Douglas went north again, this time to Great Bear Lake. Backed by the Sudbury Diamond Drilling Company, he planned to stake the coal he had seen on Douglas Bay. Now that uranium had been discovered on McTavish Bay, these deposits might become commercially important. The plan, highly secretive, involved a quick winter trip for staking and a longer summer trip for investigation.

His trip to the Coppermine in 1912 took 18 months. Now, in 1932 he left Toronto by train on February 29 to arrive in Edmonton three days later at 10:35 a.m. and flew north at noon. Punch Dickins of Canadian Airways took him out to the aerodrome where a Bellanca was waiting for him with Ronald George as pilot. As they flew over the Athabasca, Douglas, with his nose pressed to the cabin window, could recognize each rapid which cost such labour and frustration 20 years earlier. Heavy winds made for a rough ride, but they arrived safely at Fort McMurray at 2:45 that afternoon.

PLATE 81

There was considerable air activity at McMurray. Douglas knew that he was sharing an historic moment, that something was happening in the North of Canada that had happened no where else in the world.

The first airplanes to fly down the Mackenzie River were two Junkers brought in by Imperial Oil which was anxious to stake claims near the oil discovery made in 1920. They took off from Edmonton in March 1921 carrying a petroleum geologist and surveyor.

As they landed in bad weather on frozen sled ruts, one of the planes broke a ski and later, trying to take off, broke a propeller. The mechanic improvised a propeller from an oak sled runner and moose hide glue. Next they took off and crash landed at Fort Norman. The men clung to a wing tip and were rescued by canoe. Thus the story of northern flying got underway.

By 1932 flying was accepted in the North but bad weather and risk was always there and the ingenuity and adaptability of northern pilots and mechanics were becoming the stuff of legend.

> There were Five planes there,and some of the best fliers in the world. For none deserve that title more than these men flying into the north ... Walter Gilbert, Punch Dickins, Andy Cruikshank, Bill Spence and Wop May to mention some of them.[1]

'Punch' Dickins has identified the fliers lined up beneath the wing of a Bellanca Pacemaker in the Douglas photo: (left to right) unknown; Frank Barager, pilot; Casey Van Der Linden, mechanic; Jim Skeel, agent; unknown; Frank Kelly, mechanic; Archie McMullen, pilot; Walter Gilbert, pilot; Ron George, pilot; Fred Hodgins, mechanic; Al Hunt, mechanic; 'Micky' Sutherland, mechanic; Bob Porritt, W.C. agent at Fort Resolution.

PLATE 81

PLATE 82

Walter Gilbert flew Douglas on to Fort Rae with stops at Fort Smith and Fort Resolution. This was Douglas's first look at Fort Rae and he found it, "a God forsaken place if ever there was one ..."[2]

With the rest of the world sunk in the slough of the Great Depression, excitement and optimism was snapping in the cold air of the North. Four other planes loaded with prospectors and their gear were at Fort Rae following the same course to Great Bear.

The tiny restaurant run by Jim Derwash was, "... quite a sight with all these men crowded into it. The night was very cold, and the northern lights very bright in their familiar northern form of a curtain overhead."[3]

Douglas, Gilbert and Ingram, Inspector of Civil Aviation, found quarters with Constable Salket at the RCMP house. The other men slept in Derwash's restaurant.

The temperature was -40° in the morning and Walter Gilbert found he could not get his plane off the snow. They wiped a heavy layer of frost off the wings, then found that one of the shock absorbers was low. They jacked up the plane, then could not get the air pump to work because it was frozen. Next they could not get the valve to hold.

> Jacked up the wing of the plane, and took the shock absorber up to the house and thawed it out, drained the oil, and put in another valve. ... We had lunch and made another try, but couldn't hold the air, finally jacked up again, and sealed the valve with rubber solution, and took off o.k. at 3:10 p.m.[4]

PLATE 82

PLATE 83

About 10:30 p.m. on the night of July 19th, 1912, I looked eastward over the waters of Great Bear Lake, dead calm under a beautiful summer sky, bidding farewell to a lake that had treated us so kindly, and wondering when, and under what circumstances I should see them again. My wildest guess could not have approached the reality. On March 5th, 1931 about 5:30 p.m. we flew over Conjurer Bay, and along the East shore of McTavish Bay. It is a terribly rough country, high rocky hills and fearfully complex topography. It was a lovely winter evening, the sun was just setting and the lights over the wide expanse of ice were wonderful. The surface of the lake was incredibly windswept, about half polished bare ice, the rest the hardest of drifts.[5]

Walter Gilbert managed a safe but very rough landing on the great north-east arm known as McTavish Bay. Here in Echo Bay in 1930, Gilbert LaBine had discovered uranium. For Douglas, the excitement there carried a tinge of regret. In a autobiography requested by Vilhjalmur Stefansson years later, he described his investigation of the Coppermine River:

This area was then withdrawn from staking, but what I had seen in the North led me to advise James Douglas to investigate the McTavish Bay area of Great Bear Lake, and some other areas outside the bounds of the withdrawn area. I urged this to the point of importunity almost right up to the time war broke in August 1914. This of course put a temporary end to Northern exploration. At that time James Douglas was interested in the development of the Colorado carnotite [stet] fields as a source of radium, in fact he spent millions to that end. I have often thought how different the history of Great Bear Lake might have been if James Douglas had acceded to my requests. For if we had investigated the McTavish Bay area we should certainly have found the uranium at Echo Bay, and with James Douglas's interest in radium there would have been ample funds available for their development.[6]

PLATE 83

PLATE 84

Gilbert LaBine, born in the Ottawa Valley, was already a veteran of the Cobalt Silver Rush and of Eldorado Gold Mines when he arranged for Punch Dickens to fly him to Great Bear Lake in 1929. He prospected alone for three weeks finding enough bismuth, copper and cobalt to excite him. What excited him even more was a particular cliff that he had seen from the air as Punch Dickens flew him home. He said later that the colours in that tower of rock looked like an Oriental rug.

Back in Ottawa he came upon the report of J. Mackintosh Bell who, with Charles Camsell, made a remarkable exploration of the shores of Great Bear Lake in the summer of 1900. Bell's report said: "In the greenstones east of McTavish Bay occur numerous interrupted stringers of calspar containing chalcopyrite and the steep rocky shores which here present themselves to the lake are often stained with cobalt bloom and copper sheen." [7] Labine realized that that sentence described the cliff he had seen from the air but where it was he did not know. Bell's mention of McTavish Bay narrowed it down to about 800 miles of Great Bear shoreline. LaBine went back the next summer and found it. Along with silver, bismuth and cobalt, he made the find of the century: pitchblende, the source of radium and uranium.

In March 1932, Douglas found a well-built log cabin on Echo Bay.

"Jack, one of the Labine brothers was cook, he and some of the Labine crowd had come in just ahead of us. Two men had been at this camp all winter, and it was in very good shape."

There were nine men in the cabin that night. "Probably thirty or more prospectors have gone in since March 1st. These are all experienced men, mostly from around the northern Ontario camps ..."

After the depressing condition of things in 'civilization' it was most cheerful and stimulating to be with these men, who are hopefully planning, and executing their plans with vigor and intelligence. I found the fliers a particularly fine bunch of men to be with, they made me welcome in their fraternity and treated me like one of themselves. I have seen nothing like this since the early days in Arizona, when the same spirit was shown in developing a new country.

By the end of the year, the mine site had a sawmill and electric power plant, a post office and general store, RCMP post, two radio stations, a mining recorder's office, and 200 people. Such was the beginning of the town of Eldorado.

PLATE 85

Whatever the spirit of camaraderie in the LaBine cabin, it did not interfere with the secrecy maintained in the serious business of staking. "Walter and I held a council of war that night. He didn't even know where I was going I was keeping my movements so close."[8] Douglas was worried about landing conditions on Douglas Bay near Gros Cap, the most exposed point on the whole lake. The winter of 1932 had been unusually severe in the North with high winds, severe cold and twice as much snow as usual. Those winds had whipped and hardened the snow surface of Great Bear until it resembled gouged rock.

On more than one occasion in 1911-12 we had had wonderful luck on Great Bear Lake, and this luck held once more. We flew across the lake next day, and found a good landing place exactly where I wanted to be, the only good landing place within fifty miles or more.[9]

PLATE 84

PLATE 85

PLATE 87

PLATE 86

With Gilbert's help, Douglas put in a strenuous six hours of work to stake the 1450 acres of ground strictly according to regulations, then flew across to Cape McDonnel, to follow the shoreline around to LaBine Point, "... glad enough to get back to that over-warm house tonight." [10]

PLATE 87

On Monday morning, March 7, they left Labine Point and made a stop in Lindsley Bay, "... a gloomy cold place, it was 35 below here, 3 men. They had three tents, each with a stove and seemed to be pretty comfortable." [11]

   The men pictured here are Eric Beck and Ted Watt. Watt, a newspaperman from Edmonton with no northern experience, was dumped down on Great Bear with Beck in January in an attempt to beat the spring prospecting rush. His experiences were chronicled in the first dispatches to come out from the camps and were later described in a book entitled *Great Bear.* [12]

PLATE 88

In the late afternoon of March 7, only one week after he left Toronto, his plane landed at Fort Smith and Douglas had his claims in at the recording office. Went to the hotel then, had a good tea, change and shave, then visited McDougall. [13]

   With the dog team and the airplane, the North had a foot in the past and a foot in the future. Douglas enjoyed both worlds.

PLATE 88

PLATE 89

Walter Gilbert, pilot, George M.Douglas and Rudolph Heuss, mechanic, at McMurray on the way home. Douglas would refer to this trip as "a great adventure, quite the most notable adventure of my life indeed and I was sorry it was over."[14]

PLATE 90

Douglas was back at Northcote Farm to watch the Kawartha spring thaw Katchiwano Lake. By July he was in the North again watching the Arctic spring chew at the ice of Great Bear. This time he had come in the hard way, up the swift Bear River by canoe.

The Bear River saw more activity this summer than at any time in its history. Discovery Well, 51 miles north of Fort Norman, had been re-opened to provide oil for Eldorado on Echo Bay. The problem was getting it up the Bear River. Crews of men were moved in by HBC barge and power-boat to start building a road around the eight miles of rapids, " ... a fool project if ever there was one."[15] Douglas felt the money could have been better used to dredge the river channel.

PLATE 89

PLATE 90

PLATE 91

This time Douglas's heavy freight was not tracked laboriously up the Bear, but flown in to Franklin by Paul Calder of Canada Airways. Douglas and Peter Pitcher, a student from the University of Alberta, arrived in wet, cold, gloomy weather and were fortunate to get the HBC warehouse to live in during the two days it took to sort their freight.

On July 6 Douglas and Pitcher set out from Franklin using a 10-horse power engine on a 19-foot canoe especially designed and built for this trip. They planned to travel around the south-west shore of Keith Arm to Jupiter Bay where Douglas had seen "float coal" on the beach when the *Jupiter* was blown ashore during a storm in 1911.

Before they left Franklin, the forerunners of the summer stampede to Eldorado were coming in. Now three different parties followed Douglas around the shore of Keith Arm bound for Echo Bay on McTavish Arm. One was an old chap named Art Bird, who was making his way in a home-made skiff all by himself, in spite of a crippled arm. He intended to prospect and do carpentry around the Echo Bay settlement.

The *Sloan* was a small schooner skippered by Charlie Sloan, an old-timer who had been on Great Bear Lake since 1914. "He is a good sort, absolutely straight and always ready to help anyone out."[16] With a crew of three men, Charlie was making his way to the excitement at Echo Bay.

Close behind the *Sloan* was the *B.E.A.R.* (Bear Exploration and Radium), a power scow with four men on board. They were soon all stopped by ice on the lake. The *Sloan* and the *B.E.A.R.* both camped across a little creek from Douglas and Pitcher. Sloan's yarns about trading, trapping and prospecting on the lake entertained them around the campfire that night.

PLATE 92

PLATE 93

By making the trip in a canoe, they had a much more thorough look at the shores than a fly-in by plane would have allowed. Peter Pitcher, the young student who would later become manager of the Giant-Yellowknife Mine on Great Slave Lake, was a cheerful companion and willing worker.

There was float coal on Jupiter Beach again but no coal seam of interest. In ten days they travelled 250 miles and returned to Franklin.

July 17 they began their journey north to the Scented Grass Hills of Etacho Point to inspect the coal staked in March. Eight days later, after several battles with weather and rough water, they beached their canoe on Douglas Bay.

For Douglas it was a real pleasure to be back in the Barrens:, "... with its freshness and exhilaration, its scented atmosphere, its uninterrupted vision, the ease of walking and freedom of movement ..."

Their campsite was on a shelf-like elevation above an estuary. Behind them the hill rose steeply to a hundred-foot height. The view from their shelf gave them a double sunset as the sun sank behind the hill to the west about 8 p.m. and emerged at 9:30 for another hour before it set again in the lake. Then after two hours of twilight, it reappeared for a new day. "Far northern skies have a peculiar quality of immensity and serenity, the dome seems vaster than in southern latitudes: in no place have I seen more lovely skies than from our Boulder Point camp."[17]

By the end of the two weeks, they had surveyed the claim and turned back to Franklin. In a letter to Denny LaNauze, Douglas wrote: "I should like to have made the trip to Hodgson's Point when I was so comparatively close to it. But visiting these other well remembered places had an element of sadness ..."[18]

PLATE 93

PLATE 94

One delightful surprise for Douglas on this trip north was meeting D'Arcy Arden at Chipewyan. They had corresponded since 1918 and had narrowly missed meeting in 1928 to the great disappointment of both. Now after a ride in an RCMP boat, Douglas found Arden's craft tied up at the wharf. The Sergeant called him over and introduced the two men.

Later, as they visited in the cabin of the police boat, Arimo arrived with two small boys; the sergeant called her over, saying he had an old friend for her to meet. She came into the dark cabin and looked at Douglas very piercingly. When Arden said, "Don't you know him?" she shook her head slowly. Then he mentioned Hornby's name and Arimo recognized him. Douglas wrote about her to August Sandberg later:

> ... she had been married for 17 or 18 years to D'Arcy Arden, who spent about 10 years on Great Bear Lake. ... It was very funny to have a talk with this woman, who can speak good English now. She is certainly a woman of great strength of character and much humour.[19]

PLATE 94

PLATE 95

By 1935 the attention shifted from Great Bear Lake to Great Slave Lake. The previous year, a veteran prospector and explorer, Major Lockie Burwash, had staked claims near the mouth of the Yellowknife River which aroused ripples of excitement in prospecting circles. Dr A.W. Jolliffe of the Geological Survey was taking no less than seven parties to the north shore of Great Slave where, with the help of bush planes, they planned to explore 3000 square miles before the summer was over.

Gold had also been found at Beaverlodge on Lake Athabasca. Douglas, working again for United Verde of Clarkedale, Arizona, took two parties north to check out these finds, explore the unstaked country north of Lake Athabasca and follow up possibilities which he and Dr Lausen had seen in 1928. He also flew up to Great Bear to do further work on the coal claims there.

Some prospectors still relied on the traditional dog-sled for transportation. The *Canadusa*, an HBC gas powered boat on which Douglas had travelled upriver in 1932, carries 70 dogs north.

PLATE 96

"I do not believe that ever before has aerial photography been applied so carefully and exten-sively to prospecting work in an unknown country as we did in the far north in the summer of 1935."[1]

Dr C.H. Stool of the Geological Survey showed him work not yet published and Dr A.M. Narraway, Chief of Aerial Surveys, allowed him to trace partly plotted work and photograph advance maps. Douglas realized that the average prospector could not fully use this wealth of data, but he knew the man who could: Guy Blanchet.

In Douglas notes and letters, Blanchet is referred to repeatedly as a "remarkable man." The two men were often glad to part ways, but each had unbounded respect for the other's work. Blanchet was born in Ottawa in 1884, graduated from McGill in mining engineering in 1905 and became a Dominion Land Surveyor in 1907. In 1910 he joined the Topographical Survey of Canada. He met Jack Hornby several times in the 1920s; he also tried to dissuade Edgar Christian from accompanying Hornby on his last trip. In 1930 Blanchet left his government career to work independently.

Blanchet and Douglas reached Beaverlodge on Lake Athabasca by canoe. René Hansen, an experienced prospector, and Bobby Jones, a young geologist, arrived there by plane. Hansen worked with Blanchet on Athabasca Lake while Jones travelled by canoe with Douglas to Great Slave Lake to begin work there.

For a brief two hours in June, the four men met at Beaverlodge. Douglas photographed Blanchet, Hansen and Jones in a moment of relaxation.

PLATE 96

PLATE 97

Base camp for Douglas and Jones on Great Slave was on an island east of Eagle Island, the site of the fire during the 1928 trip.

From here they worked inland along the south shore, looked at unexplored country southwest of McDonnel Lake, examined country south of Stark Lake and east of the Snowdrift River, and examined the great fault that occurs along the south shore of the lake.

August 3, Douglas and Jones were back at East Island, their rendezvous for pick-up by plane. In spite of the number of people prospecting on Great Slave that summer, they had seen no-one and had no news of the outside world since June. On August 5, the date set for Jones's departure, the weather turned wild and windy. As they built a spruce wind break and watched a gust of wind take the pan of bannock out of their reflector oven and thrown it dough-side-down in the fire, they gave up looking for a plane.

Next day, sullen threatening skies lent an ominous stillness to the day. Suddenly, a Junkers came up from the west, circled and landed. "Wop May was the pilot, Lou Parmentier the mechanic. They had just flown from Fort Resolution, and Wop was anxious to get back there before it got any darker ... It was very exciting to see some one from the outside world again, especially such good friends as these... Within half an hour of the plane's landing, it had taken off again with Bobby aboard and had disappeared in the dull western sky; leaving me alone, but with a big bunch of letters as a tangible proof that this sudden intrusion of strangers in my solitude and their sudden disappearance was not some trick of the imagination."[2]

PLATE 97

PLATE 98

On August 7, as the barometer fell abnormally low, no plane arrived to pick up Douglas. He moved from the large canoe, *Pahie,* where he slept under a canvas tent, to the shore tent.

The next day the storm broke with gale force winds from the west and driving rain. His camp was on the lee side of East Island but waves swept through the channel and broke on a peninsula, driving the back wash in to deluge and wash away his campfire. He moved his fire to higher ground in front of the tent and kept it burning with dry driftwood in spite of heavy rain. Here he sat listening as, "... waves broke with thunderous shocks on the windward side of the island, splintering and chewing the driftwood on the sharp quartzite ledges, and throwing it far above high water mark."

On August 9 his solitude was broken when a Fairchild made a rough landing on the unsettled lake. "Matt Berry was the pilot, one of the first of the far northern fliers. Kelly was mechanic and proved later the principal enlivening spirit of our party. Blanchet was aboard, looking as brown as an Indian, and Jack Stark, a famous old time trapper of the far north, was coming with us as far as Fort Rae as a passenger."

At noon they took off after three attempts. On the third try, a gust of wind helped to lift the plane and they cleared the spruce trees by a few scant feet.

PLATE 98

PLATE 99

When they reached the north shore, they left the water to fly over unmapped country until they found a lake where Dr Jolliffe and three other men were at work. There was great excitement on their arrival because Jolliffe's food supply was running low and they were out of tobacco, "... as soon as the plane was made fast there was a general lighting up of cigarettes."

   To Douglas their outfit, particularly their cooking looked very poor and haphazard. "But the members of the party, all young men, seemed exuberantly well and happy." Their cook lit a fire and the nine men shared coffee and "some dreadful bannock" while they talked over their adventures, and generally enjoyed themselves. "Nothing could exceed the cheerful hospitality of this camp."

PLATE 99

PLATE 100

Guy Blanchet, A.W. Jolliffe, Jack Stark.

Jack Stark was an old-time Barren Lands trapper who often appeared in the bush wearing a suit. When they returned to Fort Rae, Douglas spent the evening talking to him about his trapping on the Barrens near the headwaters of the Coppermine.

PLATE 100

PLATE 101

On August 10, Berry flew Douglas and Blanchet from Fort Rae 300 miles to Cameron Bay on Great Bear Lake while Jack Stark waited his turn to be flown with his dogs into the Barrens.

Soon after their arrival, Punch Dickins flew in with Dr Charles Camsell, the federal deputy minister of mines, and Inspector Martin of the RCMP on board. ''These were all friends of ours, and we agreed it was a notable day for Cameron when three such real old timers of the north as Charlie Camsell, Blanchet and myself met there, and such pioneers of northern flying as Punch Dickins and Matt Berry.''

Over a meal of caribou steaks, they talked over plans to fly across the lake. ''Punch knew the lake well, he was the first pilot ever to fly across it, and was able to re-assure Matt on some of his misgivings and agreed with me on the route we should follow.''

It was a joy for Douglas to fly again over Great Bear on an afternoon, ''... of liquidly clear atmosphere ... From our great height we commanded a marvellous view. The high ridge of Etacho Peninsula, the 'Scented Grass Hills' of Franklin, terminating in Gros Cap, was plainly visible ahead of us. The Grizzly Bear Mountains on the peninsula between Keith and McVicar Bays could be seen cloudlike and ethereal far to the south... I could even make out dimly the valley of the Dease River... It was an indescribably beautiful panorama.''

PLATE 101

PLATE 102

The purpose of this trip was to reduce the number of coal stakings made in 1931, and this would be done to "Blanchet's standard of meticulous accuracy." It involved cutting a line through gullies where dense tough willows stood in two feet of swamp water. Each day before they could begin, they had a four mile hike to Boulder Point either stumbling across beach cobble stones or picking their way over the cliffs.

Berry and Kelly, the plane's mechanic, came along on the second day. Matt Berry, the pilot, "... was a hard worker and a skilful axeman. Kelly put in one day of chaining and digging ... and then passed out of the surveying picture, and there after took it easy in camp. Blanchet, as usual with him, did two men's work."

In 1932 Douglas had built a teepee at Boulder Point; now five years later he found it still standing. He also found evidence of his 1912 campsite: the remains of brush beds used then were still there after twenty years.

PLATE 102

PLATE 103

The five days of relentless drudgery were made worse for Douglas by, " ... the intolerable sloppiness of our camp and meals ..." Order was essential to him, particularly as he grew older, and he suffered without it. Blanchet had become, "... a very Indian in his disregard of non-essential amenities, such as order and system. He was a good cook, but meals to him were merely a prelude to a pipe, and to be got through as quickly as possible ... Kelly was completely indifferent to order, or cleanliness, or conservation... Matt was a good cook, and for a while he and I did our best to maintain our standards in the face of fearful odds that finally overwhelmed us."

Blanchet wrote later: "We were different in our habits. In washing dishes, George would boil two pails of water if even for one cup, one spoon. I would swish mine in the lake."[3]

To complicate matters, there was a real shortage of food. Douglas had counted on a cache left at Douglas Bay in 1932 and he found it robbed. "No Indian had done this, the Indians despise such despicable acts. Some of the low-down whites brought into the country by the 'Bear Lake Rush' had been guilty of this robbery." He had also counted on ptarmigan and rabbits; ptarmigan were scarce, rabbits not seen at all. Instead wolves were numerous and prowled around their camp at night. After Kelly managed to lose their only bait, they had no fish, so meals were mostly beans and flapjacks.

Oddly enough, Douglas remembered Kelly as the saving grace of their camp. A liability in every other way, " ...he had the saving grace of humour; like Falstaff, he was not only witty in himself, but the cause of wit in other men." So they managed to laugh at the mess they lived in and get the job done.

PLATE 103

PLATE 104

On August 15 they ate the last of their beans, and took off into rising wind and driving clouds. As the wind blew them off course to the very middle of the lake, the engine began to misfire in one of the cylinders. For an anxious hour Douglas and Blanchet stared down at the stormy sea from an altitude low enough to, "... see the angry waves to full advantage." Kelly lay on the floor reading a humourous calendar. When they landed at last on Cameron Bay, Blanchet said to Kelly, "Did you find that joke book of yours funny?"

"Oh yes, funny as hell, I was listening every beat of the engine and thinking how cold that water looked below us."

The caribou steaks at Harry Reed's place tasted extremely good that night. The radio station reported bad weather everywhere throughout the North and all planes grounded.

The weather had cleared a little at noon next day when they took off for a thoroughly unpleasant flight. Berry had a message to pick up a Survey man on a lake north-east of Fort Rae. The man had been taken in by an army plane and now the army planes had all gone south.

Douglas thought their chances of finding him just about nil. Why not fly to Fort Rae, then make a special flight with more information, or a Survey man on board who knew his whereabouts? "However I had no say in the matter; our special charter had ended on our return to Cameron Bay and now Blanchet and I were mere passengers, 'With no more say than an express parcel,' as Blanchet said."

They flew south to White Eagle Falls on the Camsell River, then out across the uncharted Barrens to search for a tiny tent on an unknown lake. They had no radio and, in Douglas's opinion, were far off course for the man's likely position. They had no food, and no prospect of finding any if forced down. The lakes below were empty of loons and ducks which indicated an absence of fish. There were no signs of animal life. Low clouds and fog were rolling in from the north. The engine was working none too well and their gas supply began to run low.

The shortage of gas forced Berry to give up and follow the Snare River to Fort Rae. They had not been within 200 miles of where the man really was.

When it cleared at noon next day Berry decided to run for East Island. The 30-mile-an-hour wind made landing difficult. "Just as we were slowing down under the lee of the island a heavy gust of wind lifted the plane off the water again. We pitched forward and had so scant a margin in which to finish our run that the tips of the propeller hit the alders on the edge of the island."

As soon as Kelly had the propeller fixed, the pilot took off in a hurry. Douglas and Blanchet settled in to their comfortable camp, made a fire and enjoyed a good meal from the ample stores cached there. That night Douglas, "... slept the deep sleep of relief from worry ... content with canoe travel and camping, and above all, glad to be done with planes, and once more master of my own movements."

PLATE 104

PLATE 105

Douglas made his last trip north in 1938, a year of frenzied excitement at Yellowknife. As he left Edmonton on May 3, the mood of boom-time bustle was evident: "It was a tremendous train, 247 passengers for Waterways, transport workers, deck hands and stevedores, carpenters and their helpers, shipbuilders etc." Waterways, three miles above McMurray, had become a ship-building centre. Swarms of men were at work in deep mud, putting up shacks and warehouses, building docks or chutes and constructing large barges to carry machinery, lumber and foodstuffs to Yellowknife.

Low water made travel on the rivers extremely difficult just as an unprecedented volume of freight had to be moved downstream. Douglas went down on the HBC's *Pelly Lake:* "I really enjoyed it coming down the Athabaska (the first time since 1911 that I've come down by HB transport). I liked the old Captain & the crowd of men."

When they neared Lake Athabasca they found Northern Transport's new *Radium Queen* hard aground with its two barges right across the channel. On the morning of May 15 they watched the *S.S. Athabaska* come out of Chipewyan and work her way toward them through the ice.

Ten miles behind them the *S.S. Northland Echo* was grounded in Big Point Channel. "At 9 (on Monday) an outboard dinghy from *Echo* made its way down to us with Micky Ryan, HB Transport Manager and then went on to Athabasca. It has been decided that she shall take *Pelly*'s big barge and passengers to Fitzgerald and *Echo*'s big barge and passengers too. *Echo* then to return to WW [Waterways] with empty barge and *Pelly* with hers. *Pelly* will have to be hauled out for repairs."[1]

Such was travel on the Athabasca in 1938.

PLATE 106

PLATE 106

On September 5 the Consolidated Mining and Smelting Company at Yellowknife poured its first gold brick. That summer prospectors radiated out across Great Slave Lake. By the end of the year 4000 claims were staked within a 200 mile radius of the town.

When the grounded *Echo* was freed and reached the *Athabaska,* she brought René Hansen who would be Douglas's partner for the summer. They left the luxurious *Athabaska* at Fitzgerald and from Fort Smith made their way by canoe to the south shore of Great Slave Lake. With difficulty they pushed east through the ice to reach the Chubun River and began exploring the "magnificent" lakes from which this river flows. After they prospected east along another 50 miles of Great Slave shoreline, they took their canoes through the islands to the north shore.

When Douglas and Hansen first saw Yellowknife in June it was a collection of tents surrounded by construction. They camped on an island where they were joined by Tom Greenland.

From their campsite, the three men watched Yellowknife rising from its rocks: "Frantic building, planes more than I've ever seen in one place before – RCAF, Can Airways, Mackenzie Airways, private planes – water taxis running between the town and the mines, bootlegging, drunkenness, idleness. But the men are alright. I knew many, and it is an interesting thing to have seen."[2]

PLATE 107

PLATE 107

Douglas, Hansen and Greenland made their way through the 90-mile maze of islands to Fort Rae. None of the trip was idyllic.

"Parts of it are a veritable nightmare ..." Douglas wrote to his wife. "You must be sick and tired of my complaints about the weather but there was an almost personal animosity in its treatment of me ..."[3]

High winds and rain lashed their outfit and made travel dangerous most of the time, impossible some of the time. Even in camp the storms threatened to destroy the *Pahie* at anchor, made it extremely hard to get any work done and made camp life a misery. At age 63, Douglas began to feel that he was too old to deal with the harshness of this land. Was it now a young man's land where he no longer belonged?

PLATE 108

The three men reached Rae at treaty-paying time to see a city of tents of at least 200 families with all their dogs. Large canoes arrived continually and the Hudson's Bay store and Northern Traders store were thronged with Indian shoppers. Everywhere was a mood of celebration.

> I have seen more of Indians and Indian life this year than on all my previous trips. The Fort Rae Dog Ribs are a fine cheerful lot, remind me of the Mexicans, cheerful and hard working.[4]

PLATE 108

PLATE 109

Tom Greenland, the young assistant, brightened the miserable rainy days and lightened the burden of work. Not a large man, he was extremely powerful and always took the heavy end of the loads. He worked well with both Douglas and Hansen.

The Snare River which they entered at Rae led to beautiful country, parklike, with spruce trees and sandy undulations covered with thick green moss. When the sun came out on the Snare, Douglas knew why he had come again to this land that could seem so God-forsaken at times.

When they came back to Yellowknife after four weeks, they sat in their canoes blinking at the transformation. A helter-skelter, hodge-podge city had replaced the tents. On July 22, a 32-room hotel had opened, just in time for the visit of Ontario Premier Mitch Hepburn. (The stairs were put in place while the Premier's plane was setting down on the bay.)

On that same day, two prospectors, Fred Thompson and Roy Lundmark, stood staring at surface gold on an island northeast of Yellowknife in the Beaulieu River area, possibly the most spectacular find of surface gold in Canadian history. When the news broke in late August, Treasure Island added fuel to the flames of excitement.

Already, in early August, Douglas saw "... brokers, dealers, stock-market gamblers, newspapers, supply houses, transport and flying companies, chambers of commerce."[5] The Wild Cat Cafe, the general stores, the barber shops and bakeries springing up here were unlike anything the North had seen before. Planes, motortugs and large barges kept the waterfront busy. There was no little island to camp on now. One island had been taken over by an airline company, another had become a lumber yard and oil cache. The three explorers turned their canoes away to find a peaceful campsite some distance from the town.

PLATE 109

PLATE 110

Tom Greenland and Ren Hansen start with Jack Stark and Gus Desteffany, two famous
old time trappers of the far north. Gus had some claims he wanted to show us.

Douglas planned to go back to the south shore for further work, but Tom Greenland had
proved so capable that he decided to send Hansen and Greenland across without him while
he boarded the HBC *Dease Lake* for a tour of Great Slave Lake. He was treating himself to
a holiday cruise.

It was a working holiday as he kept eyes and ears tuned for hints of gold. But it must have
been an idyllic time too. With the *Pahie* lashed on board, he was free from the constant planning and detailed decision-making which had always been his lot in the North, free to dream
a little, to meet old friends, tell stories and reminisce as only 'old-timers' can. Perhaps he sensed
that these would be his last days on Great Slave and he needed more than work and worry
as a memory of this remarkable inland sea.

PLATE 110

PLATE 111

The *Dease Lake* went up to Fort Smith where it loaded supplies for the Hudson's Bay posts and lumber for the building going on at Yellowknife and Rae. Pushing both a 175-ton barge and an 80-ton barge it dropped supplies at Resolution and went east to Reliance.

At Reliance ten trappers were waiting to be flown in to the Barren Lands, including Matt Murphy and the Stewart brothers, Malcolm and Allan. "It was most interesting to talk to these men, to sit in a little tent with about 5 of them and a small stove made out of a gas can while the wind blew and the rain fell outside."[6]

Inevitably the talk turned to Hornby who had become a legend on Great Bear and Great Slave. The Stewart brothers had met Hornby and Bullock during the winter of 1924-25. They told how Hornby had travelled out to Reliance and sent a letter to Corporal Hawkins at Resolution stating that he thought Bullock was insane. Hawkins set out and travelled for nine days to reach the men in the cave. He reported that Bullock appeared as normal as anyone living in such conditions could appear. But, off the cuff, he told people at Reliance that they were both plum crazy.

With the dread fascination which all Northerners feel for the subject, they talked of Hornby's death by starvation. The Stewarts, almost the last men to see Hornby alive, told Douglas they had had to coax him to take sugar, flour and tea from them. Murphy also mentioned a cache on the Casba River which the Stewarts had given Hornby permission to use; Hornby apparently had declined.

PLATE 111

PLATE 112

Douglas and Paul Beaulieu, a Dog-Rib Indian, used to cross paths occasionally from 1928 to 1938. As a young man, Paul had acted as a guide for Warburton Pike; his grandfather had guided Franklin.

In 1932 Douglas was on his way down the Slave River to Resolution. Beaulieu's party of Indians were on their way up, but their outboard engine had broken down about 100 miles below Smith, " ... and they were out of grub. I gave the old man half a side of bacon, flour, tea, tobacco and a pipe."[7]

Now he met Paul again at Fort Smith and took this picture of him with his family and power scow.

PLATE 112

PLATE 113

On this trip, Douglas met Prentice Downes, an American schoolteacher and northern wanderer. Downes had travelled that summer on the Mackenzie river and on Great Bear Lake; he had flown from Great Bear to Yellowknife and now was crossing to Resolution on a barge pulled by the *Dease Lake*. In his diary Downes recorded that they got away about six in the morning; he then described his first impression of Douglas:

> As the various inhabitants of the boat emerged into the daylight, one particularly striking person was immediately obvious. A very tall gentleman, with snow-white hair and moustache, tanned a leathery brown, with extraordinarily bright blue eyes under shaggy white eyebrows. A jutting chin, and beak of a nose. I recognised him immediately from a portrait painted 28 years ago – George Douglas, the hero and author of *Lands Forlorn*, his account of his trip across Great Bear Lake to the Coppermine and the Arctic coast so many years ago [1911-12], an account which I prize among my northern books. He was washing a pair of khaki pants, some underwear and socks, and had the biggest wrists and the kindliest smile of anyone I have ever met.
>
> I followed him about from washtub to clothesline, which he had strung away at the forward end of the forward barge, like a dog, and must have been a perfect nuisance. Our talk was of course all North. Curiously, Douglas absolutely shut up when I asked about Hornby. ... He must have been a very powerful man – a very large-boned man today but somewhat stooped with age, though very light on his feet and extremely active.

Later that day Downes wrote: "All day Douglas has been climbing about, training his glasses on the islands, identifying this one and that with all the zest of a youngster."[8]
Douglas was 63 that summer and Downs was 29. The two men played chess, talked and began a friendship that was to last for twenty years.

PLATE 113

PLATE 114

At Yellowknife Douglas took pictures around the Consolidated Mining Company site, "... a good lay out but sad to see in this country."

He left again on the morning of August 25 and his comments in a letter home sum up his impressions: "You would have been amused if you had seen the way we got off from YK with all the crew but the Captain and Engineer and leading seaman dead to the world, even the Pilot they took had gone under. YK is the most visibly drunken place I have ever seen ..."[9]

The quest that began for Douglas with his brother, Lionel, and August Sandberg in the great lonely space of Coppermine country ended here with this final image of a drunken Yellowknife celebrating the discovery of gold instead of copper.

Douglas himself would not share the great riches. The last sentence of his 1938 report to United Verde says, "I regret to say that our season's work must be regarded as barren, and I am not even prepared to make any recommendation as a result of it."[10]

Cap. 12

The *Pahie's* last anchorage on Great Slave Lake at Fort Resolution.

PLATE 114

PLATE 115

Chapter 18
Fellow Travellers

Indians appear sporadically in the books of northern history, all written by white men. They are little more than names and the stories are never told from their point of view. They don't leave written opinions of the white man they travel with; often they don't even speak his language. But a few native names ring out so repeatedly from the pages of the explorers, that they take on bodies and personalities. A student of the sub-Arctic like Douglas would have heard the name Beaulieu long before he met a member of the clan.

The genteel background of George Douglas set him a long way apart from Paul Beaulieu whose ancestors lived the hard roving life of Chipewyan hunters. In 1911, Douglas's opinion of Indians as expressed in *Lands Forlorn* was quite explicit:

> The Indians of the Mackenzie River valley have earned a most unenviable character for thorough unreliability and inefficiency. All travellers who have accomplished anything agree in describing them as worthless, shiftless, careless, unreliable, and generally contemptible.

The friendship that grew between him and Beaulieu in the 1930s suggests that 25 years of northern experience had radically changed his opinions.

In 1932 Douglas gave the old man grub on the Slave River. In 1938 the two met on what would be Douglas's last trip North. Old Paul was also expecting to leave the North for good. In a letter written later that year Douglas said, "An old Indian chief up in the far north ... who was with Pike in 1891 told me this summer that he was now 83 and did not want to live any longer, that now Jesus wasn't boss any more that the Devil was boss now."[1]

P.G. Downes, Douglas's travelling companion on the *Dease Lake,* knew the Indians between the Mackenzie River and Hudson Bay better than almost any other white man. He spoke Cree and some Chipewyan; he had travelled and lived with Indians for several summers. He had also read the history of the fur-trade extensively and had a rare ability to see it from the Indian point of view.

Downes and Douglas met Paul Beaulieu after they reached Fort Smith. Downes, who had never seen the man before but knew all about him, described that meeting later:

> ... I was camped on the banks of the Slave River and a tattered old Dog-Rib Indian walked by whom I invited to tea. In the somewhat difficult process of our conversation I asked him his name. I nearly jumped out of my skin when he told me who he was. The Beaulieus are one of those native or half-breed families who over generations repeat the same arduous and unsung behaviour, unappreciated and relatively unrewarded -- the sinews if not the brains of northern trips.[2]

Paul Beaulieu's grandfather had travelled with David Thompson, Alexander Mackenzie and Franklin. His family history provides an alternative view of northern exploration. His family name itself resulted from white encroachment on native territory. As he told Douglas: "The father of my grandfather was a Frenchman of the Brigade. He spent a night at Chipewyan, that was the start of my family."[3]

Guy Blanchet, whose Indian pilot was a Beaulieu, gave a brief account of Dog-Rib history in a 1926 government publication:

When the district was first known, the Yellowknives were the most powerful people and claimed the best caribou passes and the most productive fisheries, but about 1830 the Dog-ribs rose against them and nearly exterminated the tribe and they never recovered from this reverse. The Dog-ribs to-day seek to isolate themselves from outside influences, and retain many of their customs and the independent life of their forefathers. They inhabit the country of the north arm of Great Slave lake, westward to lac la Martre, northerly to the vicinity of Great Bear lake, and northeasterly to the Coppermine river. A number of families also spend much of the year in the country of upper Taltson river. They are good hunters and trappers and the fur collection shipped from Rae, where they trade, is amongst the most valuable in the north.[4]

Paul's grandfather, François Beaulieu, was born sometime before 1778 and died in 1872, reputed to be 100 years and some days old. In 1820 Franklin reported his presence at Fort Chipewyan, where he advised the explorer on his route to the Arctic:

> [We] received from one of the North-West Company's interpreters, named Beaulieu, a half-breed who had been brought up amongst the Dog-ribbed and Copper Indians, some satisfactory information, which we afterward found tolerably correct, respecting the mode of reaching the Copper-mine River, which he had descended a considerable way, as well as of the course of that river to its mouth.[5]

Beaulieu advised that Franklin find guides from the Copper (Yellowknife) tribe as they had at times pursued the river all the way to the coast when making war on Inuit. He also told Franklin that he should establish a base at the east end of Great Bear from which he could reach the Coppermine River by four small lakes and portages. This was good advice which Franklin could not take because he needed a base nearer the fur-trading forts in order to obtain further supplies. (It was advice which George Douglas would follow almost a hundred years later in 1911.)

Franklin's party travelled by the Yellowknife and Coppermine rivers to the sea coast where they lingered too long. All endured great suffering and several of the party died of starvation before they regained Fort Providence on Great Slave Lake.

On his second journey, Franklin did establish a base on Great Bear Lake. Fort Franklin was built on Keith Arm near the Bear River from which the Mackenzie could be easily reached and followed to the sea. Beaulieu spent the winter of 1825-26 there, leading hunting expeditions to supply the fort with meat and advising Franklin on travel plans. His knowledge of the Dease River / Coppermine country saved the eastern detachment of Franklin's party 1000 miles of travel. After Dr John Richardson and Ernest Kendall explored the coast from the Mackenzie to the Coppermine, they ascended the Coppermine, then trekked overland to the mouth of the Dease where Beaulieu met them with supplies and a bateau to carry them across Great Bear to Fort Franklin.

To the facts Douglas knew, Downes added the anecdotes and legends which revealed François as a tireless traveller who moved across the whole face of the Athabasca / Great Slave / Great Bear terrain as if in his own backyard. In the tradition of his French voyageur father and using the skills of his Indian heritage, he acquired an amazing knowledge of geography. At 70 years of age he was baptised by Bishop Taché and gave up six of his seven wives, keeping the one with no teeth as he did not think that Jesus would want an Indian with no teeth. In 1862 Father Petitot met him and put his age at 85 years.

By the turn of the century King Beaulieu, son of François, was equally well known in the North. Downes said all white travellers described him as a bully and a dreadful man boastful of a mysterious medal which he claimed to have received from Queen Victoria. Warburton Pike, the big game hunter, provided the most graphic portrait of King Beaulieu and his son Paul in his book of northern adventures, published in 1917. The 28-year-old Pike met King at Fort Smith in 1889 and decided he could not manage a trip into the Barrens without him:

Nobody could give him a very good character but as he was known as a pushing fellow and first-rate traveller, besides having made a successful musk-ox hunt in the previous year, I concluded that my best chance lay in going with him. Certainly, with all his faults, I must say that he was thoroughly expert in all the arts of travel with canoes or dog-sleighs, quick in emergencies, and far more courageous than most of the half-breeds of the Great Slave Lake. When I was alone with him I found him easy enough to manage; but his three sons, who accompanied us, are the biggest scoundrels I ever had to travel with ...

The sons were François, Jose and Paul – the same Paul who met Downes and said goodbye to Douglas fifty years later on the same river.

According to Pike, a Beaulieu was "... not a nice man to travel with, as he always keeps a longing eye on his master's possessions, even though he is fully as well equipped himself, and is untrustworthy if you leave anything in his charge."[6]

As Downes sat with 83-year-old Paul drinking tea, dumfounded to have met a native who guided Warburton Pike, he asked him what he thought of the great explorer. Old Paul Beaulieu answered with no hesitation, "The worst g... d... liar I ever knew."[7] For once a northern native had his chance to put a direct opinion into the courts of history.

Pike described Paul's father, King Beaulieu, as subject to fits of violent passion, " ... so uncontrollable that he is capable of anything." Yet when he travelled with the whole family – 20 people and 15 hungry dogs -- Pike preferred to live with King as his lodge was always the quietest. The Beaulieu camp " ... was the scene of one continuous wrangle; sometimes they would quarrel with me and sometimes among themselves, but we never did anything without having a row."

When the party reached Fond du Lac, Pike and the Beaulieus decided to leave the main body of women, children, and a few men on the lake to fish while they headed out on the 300-mile expedition into the land of the musk-ox. The picked crew consisted of King, his wife and daughter; his sons, François, Jose and Paul; another 12-year-old son named Baptiste; a son-in-law named Michel; and one other small boy. They were out of food almost as soon as they left, depending on caribou for survival.

They travelled through a series of small lakes to reach Lake Camsell where they did kill caribou. From a base camp on this lake, Pike, King, Paul and François searched for musk-ox. Michel and Jose started with them but turned back to Fond du Lac. They were extremely discontent and quarrelsome, and Pike was glad to see them go.

Late in September they reached Lac de Gras and crossed the Coppermine near its headwaters. Because it was a favourite swimming place for the caribou, this place had been a point of contention between warring Dog-Rib and Yellowknife Indians. On September 27, Pike killed one musk-ox; Paul got another one later.

On the return trip King built an ice-raft of poles and paddles with the birch canoe on top to protect it from sharp breaking ice. On this, they safely travelled back over lakes where thin ice was forming. Pike was forced to admire his skill:

> Of course he had had fifty years' experience in northern travel, but he was certainly, in my opinion, far above the average of the many other half-breeds and Indians who had been my companions in more or less difficult journeys in various parts of Canada.

After they reached the tree-line, Paul and François were sent back to Fond du Lac for dog-sleighs. On Lake Camsell, Pike waited with King's family as snow began to fall and wildlife migrated south, ptarmigan in their thousands, and wolves, wolverine and Arctic foxes on the move with the caribou. Caribou came at first in scattered bands; then came "la foule": Pike was treated to the spectacle of the vast herd and for six nights heard the curious clatter of their continuous passing.

Now Pike experienced the euphoria which pervaded an Indian camp when the caribou surrounded it. In long campfire discussions over pipes, King questioned Pike on the doings of the white man in the Grand Pays, the Hudson's Bay Company, and the Queen. His words ring from Pike's account with clarity and sharpness:

> 'No,' he said, 'she may be your Queen, as she gives you everything you want, good rifles and plenty of ammunition, and you say that you eat flour at every meal in your own country. If she were my Queen, surely she would send me sometimes half a sack

of flour, a little tea, or perhaps a little sugar, and then I should say she was indeed my Queen. As it is I would rather believe Mr Reid of Fort Providence, who told me once that the earth went round and the sun stood still; but I myself have seen the sun rise in the morning and set at night for many years. It is wrong of you White Men, who know how to read and write, to tell lies to poor men who live by the muzzle of their guns.'

On November 10 Paul and Francois returned with Michel and several Indians including a Yellowknife chief named Zinto. Paul was the only Beaulieu to keep the promise the family had made to accompany Pike for the whole season. So, the next day, Paul, Pike, Zinto, Michel and five other Yellowknife Indians along with their dogs to haul supplies, struck further north to seek musk-ox.

Old King hurled abuse at Pike as they parted, "... but gave me his own hair-coat and a new pair of snow-shoes, of which I was badly in want."

Pike and King Beaulieu were two eccentric characters bound together by their quest for musk-ox and by the fight to survive cold and starvation. For five months they travelled together, quarrelling, sometimes deriding each other but also measuring skill against skill. Their mutual dislike was sometimes interrupted by begrudging respect that came close to admiration.

Pike, Paul and the others hunted successfully, slaughtered many musk-ox and returned safely to Fond du Lac. "I think for a few minutes they were really glad to see us back safe, but soon the old complaints began." After the group returned to Resolution, the settling up began: Pike believed he paid them much more than agreed upon, and the Beaulieu family claimed he paid them much less.

From the portage at Smith, Jose (brother of King) took over the party, travelling now by skiff. Pike's plan was to follow the Peace River, cross Rocky Mountain Portage and reach Fort McLeod. Jose and a deaf-and-dumb half-breed known as Dummy agreed to go with him into unknown country. They turned back finally at Fort Vermilion. Jose made a good-bye speech in the best Beaulieu tradition of eloquence:

God made the mountains, the lakes, and the big rivers. What is better than drifting down Peace River singing hymns? You are going up-stream to cross the big mountains back to your own country; I am going down-stream to marry Dummy's sister; I shall think of you many times.[8]

Pike did not fare well without them. His party became lost and was close to death by starvation on December 27 when they staggered back to the trading post at the foot of the Rocky Mountains which they had left a month ago.

Meanwhile, back on the Slave River and the shores of Great Slave Lake, the Beaulieu family thrived. When Guy Blanchet arrived in 1921 to survey and map Great Slave Lake, King's son Jose became his pilot and guide. Jose (also called Souci or Sousie) was then over 70 years old.

When Douglas, Downes and Paul Beaulieu were camped on the banks of the Slave River in 1938, Paul was tired of this life and cross at his wife:

He was in a great rage against the world in general and his wife in particular, who wishes to stay at Smith while he wishes and intends to go to Rocher River. ...The old man is most remarkable, considering the misadventures he must have had. One finger on his right hand is twisted almost in reverse from being caught in a flywheel. One wrist has been broken and is badly misshapen. He was shot through the groin yet he gets about in good shape with the aid of a cane.[9]

Before old Paul bid Douglas good-bye, he gave him his firebag as a gift, a powerful symbol of a fragile bond achieved between two very different people. The Dog Rib people sometimes referred to caribou as their mother, fire as their father. Douglas had once given Beaulieu food, the first gift of life. Now Beaulieu offered Douglas fire, the other necessity for survival in the cold North.

Chapter 19
Douglas and Downes: Northern Support

Douglas never met Beaulieu again after 1938 but his new friendship with Downes grew stronger. At Fort Smith, Downes waited for water transportation and finally had to fly out while Douglas remained, looking for Greenland and Hansen to come in from their prospecting, then sorting and packing freight. He finally took passage on the *Radium Queen*. He reached Edmonton on September 24 and wrote a letter to Downes the next day, starting a correspondence which lasted until Downes's death twenty-one years later.

Downes did not profess to be a writer but his journals, letters and his book, *Sleeping Island*, provide marvelous insight into a culture usually seen only obliquely in the diaries of northern travellers.

> I always set out alone and I experienced most of the big lakes and rivers; Great Bear, the Slave, the Mackenzie, the Yukon, the Barrens, Labrador, Baffin Island, Ellesmere. I remember one time after a dreadful trip, camping on the edge of the tree line, again it was one of those indescribable smokey, bright-hazy days one sometimes gets in the high latitudes. I had hit the caribou migration and there was lots of meat; it was a curious spot for all the horizon seemed to fall away from where I squatted and I said to myself; Well, I suppose I shall never be so happy again.[1]

The summer of 1938 was not a particularly happy one for him. He was recovering from what he called, "... a romantic, unrequited love affair ..." which ended when the woman was killed in a train accident. In his travel diaries he is haunted by that loss and by a sense of being unlucky in love and personal friendships. To be on the move across the North seemed to ease the loneliness.

Downes's wanderlust took him by canoe from Ile la Crosse to Waterways, travelling with Cree, then Chipewyan, Indians. At Waterways he chose to buy a canoe and paddle alone down the Athabasca and Slave to Fitzgerald. He crossed the portage to Fort Smith, then rode on the barge of the *Radium King* to Great Bear Lake's Eldorado. Coming home, he flew to Yellowknife, then travelled on the *Dease Lake* where he met Douglas.

His notes reflected his depression and a constant search for direction. He was so strongly attracted to the North and to alone-ness that he sometimes felt unfit for the outside world. "I could not help but wonder if for me all this was not the best thing after all: wandering, wandering alone, a good canoe and outfit. I do not seem to be lucky when my life entangles itself with those of other people."

But in spite of himself, Downes could not shut out the world of other people. Another woman, Edna Grace, appeared in his dreams, disrupting the perfect alone-ness he sought. At Waterways there was news from her. "The letter from E.G. was a great lift to me. As the Crees say, a man never gets lost and always comes back if he has a 'nitchimos.'"

On the canoe trip to Fort Smith his spirits reached their lowest ebb. He was short on money and ate only one meal a day, sometimes only bannock and tea. He had infection in one leg. There was no more mail from Edna Grace. While he waited for transportation at Fort Smith, camping in the rain and cold, he wrote:

Also I feel poorly, very low, probably because I am not moving, and also because I had no mail. I had expected a letter from E.G. Why ... why, when I try so hard to make myself independent of everything, of every possible tie, do I fail? Can people ever live alone with their dreams?

Personal comfort was never of great importance to him. Much later Douglas acquired what he referred to as "P.G. Downes's kitchen": a tobacco tin in which he cooked whatever he happened to have. Douglas once compared him to Diogenes who travelled only with a cup and who, when he saw a man drinking from a river, threw it away. Downes travelled light and, if food was not readily available, he did not eat.

This poor diet may have contributed to his depression and to the infected leg which was slow to heal. In his attempt to live in his mind "alone with his dreams," Downes barely kept body and soul together. His emotions swung from the joy of being alone to a desperate need for human contact. He even contemplated having a young Indian woman travel with him. He was unsure about returning to go back to teaching in the fall but recorded in his diary his determination to make it home anyway. On a day when he was feeling particularly low, he wrote: "If anything should happen to me, there are only three people I care to know it – the Rands and E.G."

Not surprisingly, Downes was strongly drawn to the Hornby legend and sought information about him from anyone in the North who knew him. "More and more I can glimpse what drove Hornby on ..." While running a series of rapids on the Slave River, he wrote, "Travelling, you are always aware of being alive – or perhaps I should say, aware of the imminence of death; not that you are scared, you are just so keenly aware of it." Such constant movement seemed to furnish a sense of purpose to Hornby, Downes and people like them whose lives lacked a clear direction.

When Downes met Douglas at Yellowknife, one of his first questions was about Hornby. Douglas, tired of being asked about Hornby, at first refused to answer. It soon became apparent to Downes that Douglas himself might provide some answers. Here was a man who had felt the powerful pull of the solitary life of the North, but who had managed to remain part of the other, "civilized" world. In his diary he praised the older man:

Here is an example of the extraordinary spry activity of D. We stopped at the mouth of the Slave to take on stove wood. The crew, of course, undertook this task; when up the narrow board walk slowly comes D. lugging a huge log on his shoulder. An amazing old gentleman, and absolutely no one's fool.[2]

Douglas's example provided Downes with a pattern, a kind of map which showed a possible route his own life might follow: "The meeting with Douglas has certainly been the high point of the return and an extraordinary break of fortune for me." Through correspondence and visits to Northcote, he and Douglas remained friends for the next twenty years.

On September 7 just before flying out, Downes wrote, "I have been happy as a bird in my little camp here. ... Someday, shackled down somewhere, how I will think longingly of this little camp on the Slave at the 60th parallel."

The next summer, after a winter of teaching school, Downes headed north from Pelican Narrows in northern Saskatchewan to Reindeer Lake where he had been twice before. He then pressed on to Neultin Lake on the edge of the Barrens, a lake mentioned by Hearne in his account of his Coppermine journey in 1771. In his book, *Sleeping Island,* Downes tried to explain the purpose of his trips:

> Sometimes I have collected folklore and legends, or have mapped routes and lakes. Always there has been the study of topography; once there was the collecting of data on various geological phenomena. There is even, in moments of profound introspection, the thought that among my ancestors were followers of Boone through Cumberland Gap and later a 'forty-niner. There is a background of reading of almost all the historical northern accounts.

A remarkably strong bond – "the powerful pull of friendship" – existed between Downes and the northern Indians:

> How could I not go back to the big lake, where one evening, with a sizzling moose heart on a stick, an old Chipewyan said, 'Stay with us. It is strange for one so white, but you know some things that only old men should know. Maybe you are a born-twice and used to be here among us once?'

Downes was able to understand the attitude of a Cree or a Chipewyan Indian faced with the insensitivity of most white explorers:

> If many white men had any idea of what utter fools they appear in the eyes of the Indians, what distressingly embarrassing personal observations are made about them, and how completely pierced is their cloak of disdain and superiority, their life would be unbearable.

Downes went on to describe the joy he felt when travelling with the Indians:

> I was glad to be travelling with Indians once more. Not the least of the pleasures of travelling with them is their immediate response to the country. Pointing out and commenting on the shapes of islands or hills, spotting ducks or birds, trying to imitate the cries of gulls and terns – all the hundreds of small things which make up the world about one they seemed to appreciate. This is a quality lacking in most white travellers. I had a particularly stimulating feeling that we were getting somewhere, getting on. There was no dallying or painful exploration of the portages; everything was rushed over, the onerous business done with once and for all and as quickly as back and legs could stand it. There was little respite in the paddling. We forged on and on.

In another scene, he painted an unforgettable picture of natives as hunters and fur traders. At Misty Lake they met the main body of the Barren Land band of Chipewyan Indians moving south with their furs:

> There was something strange, dark and splendidly barbaric about the whole thing. Children rushed about for sticks, and the camp fires were stoked up. The sky in back of the camp was a dull, sulphurous yellow with black clouds. The women, in their red silk bandannas, shrieked and clubbed at the dogs. The men were wild and shaggy, their long coarse black hair matted about their heads. ...
>
>   It occurred to me that few white men in recent years had seen quite such a thing – the last little fragment of these truly wild and nomadic northern hunters in their own

country in their thousand-year-old migration to the south. It was a picture I knew I should never forget. Here was none of the timid, white-shirt, silk-handkerchief show of the trading post gathering, the servile lounging around the Company store, the wheedling, ingratiating begging of the impoverished and misfit. Here they were free, here they were the hunters, here they were men and we were the timid strangers; we were the askers and they the givers. Remnants, proud remnants of a departed great host, like the caribou, they were moving south from the Barrens to the unknowing death that waits all free animals at the hands of the white man.

In 1940 Downes made the first of several visits to Northcote Farm. The two friends had some great talks about the North in general and about Downes's past summer in particular. Downes described his meetings with Inland or Caribou Inuit whose lives were tied entirely to the caribou herds, who knew nothing of the coastal life of the Copper Inuit. Near Windy Lake, he and his Indian companions had come upon a tent and heard talking in a strange tongue. Neither of the Indians would get out of the canoe until he went ashore to establish friendly relations. Ghosts of the old fear remained here even in 1939. "Their complete isolation had protected them from the inroads of the missionaries, and so they pursued their independent primitive life and thoughts happily and without confusion and improvement."[3]

Douglas and Downes, enjoying themselves like schoolboys, had a good paddle down Katchiwano Lake to Lakefield as the ice went out, watching huge flocks of ducks. Then Downes was off to the North to try to reach Kasba Lake on the Kazan River.

The remoteness of his route caused Douglas some concern. When the summer ended without any letter, he wrote to Denny LaNauze as he had once written about Hornby, mentioning where Downes had gone so that a quick inquiry or search could be started if no news was heard.

But Downes did come back at the end of each summer to civilization and his teaching job at Belmont Hill School in Boston. During the Second World War he left teaching and joined the cartography division of the Institute of Geographic Exploration at Harvard on contract to the Air Force.

By 1941 Downes was living in Washington, married to a "... marvelously tempestuous and talented person." He referred to this period as "the two wars."[4] While he worked for the Air Force, he and his new wife fought at home. Finally they separated, the war ended, and Downes retired to an old farm in Vermont where he lived alone for half a year.

In his letters to Douglas, Downes compared his life to the life at Northcote Farm. But Downes's life lacked the control and orderliness of the Douglas home. He began to neglect his health again, forgetting to eat properly; eventually he got scurvy. This forced him back into a Boston hospital where doctors were amazed to see a modern-day scurvy case in a New England schoolteacher. After his recovery he went back to teaching again.

In 1949, Downes married Edna Grace, whose letters in the summer of 1938 had kept him from cutting off all ties with the outside world. Their daughter Anne was born in 1950. Two years later Douglas became the godfather of their son, Nicholas: "I am much flattered at your suggestion I should be godfather to your boy, a quite strange office for me and I hesitate to accept the responsibility. K (Frances) says I should do so! so that goes."[5]

In their correspondence Douglas and Downes re-lived their northern adventures. Family life had curtailed Downes's wanderings, and Douglas was now quite elderly. Downes often wrote about his Indian friends; Douglas shared his concern for them:

> By 1928 the old contempt for the white man which was so evident to all travellers
> right up to the time I first went into the country in 1911 was no longer evident. ...
> I found the changed attitude of the Indians quite pathetic. These were mostly Dog
> Ribs and I liked the Dog Ribs best of the Indians in my limited experience of them.[6]

Downes tried to share with Douglas his attempts to understand the Cree culture. In 1954 he wrote seven pages of discourse on dreams to Douglas and apologized for his inability to fit these Indian truths into English words. "Maybe someday someone will make this 'translation' gap which I am trying to do for you."[7]

It is obvious to Downes that the sort of knowledge he has of northern natives cannot be shared with everyone. In *Some Sidelights ... Very Dim ...On History,* he told a story that revealed both his sense of humour and his distance from the "civilized world":

> In 1947 I went back to the North and walked into a bush-flyer's office asking for some photos I thought they might have of a certain lake. His efficient and youthful secretary was most obliging. As I was about to leave she said, 'You know, years ago there was a fellow who went to that lake. He is probably dead now but he wrote a book about it and at least you can get a lot of information about this spot from it.' 'Is that so?' I mildly queried. 'What did you think about it or more particularly him?' 'Mad, completely cuckoo if you ask me,' she replied. 'I agree one hundred per cent,' I replied, and then as I closed the door on the modern age, murmured, 'I know him so well.'[8]

Downes knew he needed the stability and common sense that he saw in Douglas. In return Douglas valued and learned from the younger man's insight into the native way of life. Through Downes, that culture came slowly and dimly into focus for Douglas,

Downes died of a heart attack in 1959. He was 49 years old. He had often tried to write down what he knew of Cree dreams for Douglas. In *Sleeping Island* he quoted an old Dog-Rib Indian:

> 'Tell me, Father, what is this white man's Heaven?'
>
> 'It is the most beautiful place in the world.'
>
> 'Tell me, Father, is it like the land of the little trees when the ice has left the lakes? Are the great musk oxen there? Are the hills covered with flowers? There will I see the caribou everywhere I look? Are the lakes blue with the sky of summer? Is every net full of great, fat white-fish? Is there room for me in this land, like our land, the Barrens? Can I camp anywhere and not find that someone else has camped? Can I feel the wind and be like the wind? Father, if your Heaven is not all these, leave me alone in my land, the land of the little sticks.'[9]

That Indian was speaking to Father Petitot, the priest who ventured into the Barren Lands in 1864. Jean Paul Beaulieu would have understood his sentiments, and so would George Douglas.

Chapter 20
Impossible Dream

The advent of the First World War forced Douglas to cancel his plans to go back to the Coppermine; the Second World War ended his northern travel altogether. By the time it was over he was 70. During the war he shared Lionel's grief when his oldest son, Pierce, was killed at Tobruk; after the war he watched some aspects of the world outside the gates of Northcote change beyond recognition.

But at Northcote Farm in the Kawartha Lakes, change was kept at bay. The Douglases lived to their own tune, a rhythm of the seasons unspoiled by the noise of appliances or machines. Engines and motors belonged in mines and industry; in his personal life, Douglas had no need of them.

The journalist Richard Finnie, whose father was Director of the Northwest Territories and Yukon Branch of the federal government, found the Douglas life-style eccentric but so attractive that he came to visit again and again.

Although George was a trained engineer and geologist, abreast of modern technology and exceptionally versatile in knowledge and talent, his life style veered toward the

19th century. He had outboard motors but always preferred to paddle or sail his many canoes. He had a car (a 1927 Hudson) but he avoided driving it. He bicycled, walked, snowshoed, skied or sailed according to seasonal conditions whenever he could.[1]

Mrs Douglas saw nothing unusual in the plain life they led:

If it was simple it was because we preferred it that way. For fuel we bought coal and cord wood – what we called 'wildwood' for summer use, we gathered. For lighting we bought coal oil; water came by the pail from the lake. Not until 1950 was there a telephone. We had a car about 1932 which I did not drive nor wish to ... my husband preferred the bicycle. There were time-consuming chores, but with no deadlines we could enjoy the life around us. Without being naturalists, we watched the animals and the plant life. The weather of course was important, it dictated what we did today or had better put off until tomorrow... As for other activities there were the canoes to care for, photography and letterwriting. I did some water colour painting and had quite a garden. We both read a great deal, books and many periodicals. As for food we both had very simple tastes; our clothes I patched.[2]

The life the Douglases led was also nomadic. According to the season, the weather or their mood, they moved from the Big House to the Tool House to the Floater or to one of the islands they owned in Stoney Lake. The Tool House was one of two very old log dwellings built in the 1840s. The Floater was a houseboat.

Sing Kettle (or Syndicate) Island at the upper end of Stoney Lake had flat smooth rock and reminded George of the islands in Great Slave Lake. "K [Frances] loves the place; the water is clear up at that end of the lake and the bathing is wonderful. To make a trip there by canoe, spend the night and a lazy next morning, and then come away again is a favourite program for both of us."[3]

Wee Island, a half-acre piece of rock and soil in Stoney Lake, had a small cabin which Douglas had built in 1915 after his stint at the Armstrong Works in England during the First World

War. Here he had lived alone that winter, gathering the seclusion of the islands around him as if seeking to recapture some of the solitude and sanity he associated with the cabin on Great Bear Lake. In later years he loved the island, particularly if he was alone:

> When I'm alone there, I can look on and be amused at what I see across the bay. But as soon as K arrives people land on us, or carry on a long conversation across the bay, or tie up at our wharf in a canoe to spend hours *talking* which is what they love to do among themselves.[4]

As Douglas grew older he grew less tolerant of the modern world. In 1952 he wrote to P.G. Downes:

> On what common ground can I, who walk 3 miles to get some potatoes, who reads the best English papers (or Thoreau!), meet people who take the latest model car if they have to go half a block, whose pampered life is supported by a war economy, whose idea of social entertainment is a cocktail party of 30 or more in space inadequate for 6 and the air thick with cigarette smoke ...what the devil would I do in that galley?[5]

The Douglases had no children so there were none of the usual family cares or delights to distract him. Frances was convivial by nature and she played second mother to her sisters' children. But Douglas was partially deaf and the presence of people talking at him often confused and irritated him. He found an easier way to communicate: through his pen he could talk to whomever he chose; he could dispel loneliness without strain. It is not surprising that he chose to talk to Northerners about the North. His correspondence to and about people and events in the Canadian North amounts to a library of first hand Arctic and sub-Arctic experience.

Rural mail delivery began after the Second World War. Before that, Douglas made a twice-weekly trip to Lakefield by bicycle to get the mail. Letters came from D'Arcy Arden, Denny LaNauze, Guy Blanchet, Bishop Breynat at Fort Smith, Vilhjalmur Stefansson, P.G. Downes, Richard Finnie and government men in Ottawa like M.G. Cameron, A.M. Narraway and Hugh

Spence; all talked of that "great lone land."

However much each man's personal philosophy of life varied, each respected the other for the simple fact that he had survived in the demanding conditions of the far North; and loved him as a brother because he too loved that inexplicably wonderful land which could make a man feel reborn.

Each man approached the challenge of Arctic survival in his own personal style. Some succeeded. Some failed. In *My Life With the Eskimo* published in 1913, Vilhjalmur Stefansson wrote:

> An adventure is a sign of incompetence ... If everything is well managed, if there are no miscalculations or mistakes, then the things that happen are only the things you expected to happen, for which you are ready and with which you can therefore deal.[6]

Few explorers fit Stefanssons's dictum as well as George Douglas. His method was not to charge into the North and suffer as a great many figures in the history of Arctic and sub-Arctic exploration have done: his method was to engineer every aspect of an expedition and to reach his goal in relative comfort. He was a man who delighted in a job well done, who planned to perfection and executed a task with precision and skill. Essentially he worked alone, planning and leading each expedition, the others who were with him, followed.

As late as 1943 when he was 68, he still dreamed of a trip north:

> I should like to travel across from the Western end of the Dismal lakes to about the headwaters of the Haldane, then south west to Great Bear and explore the "Good Hope Bay" as the western extension of Smith Bay is called. ... I have *twice* been balked by bad weather from doing so ... once by canoe in 1932, and again by plane in 1935. I tried last year to get enough interest to finance a trip there, but it was a total failure! and now I don't suppose I shall ever do so. Like the French peasant in Nadaud's verses:
>
>   '*Mon voeu ne s'accomplira pas*
>   *Je n'ai jamais vu Carcassonne*'[7]

In later years he was regarded as an accurate source of information for students of the Arctic who needed to get their facts straight. He wrote book reviews and letters to Clifford Wilson of the Glenbow Foundation, to *The Beaver* and to Diana Rowley, editor of *Arctic Circle*. In 1954 Vilhjalmur Stefansson, in letters to the *Royal Geographical Journal* and *The Beaver*, acknowledged the debt he felt he owed to Douglas and urged the editors to get Douglas to write articles for them:

> I have been feeling guilty, off and on these many years, about hoarding in my correspondence files otherwise unobtainable: personally gained field information, book-derived scholarship and wisdom distilled from these and other sources, all these and more having come to me through letters Douglas has written me, often in reply to questions, and through carbons he has sent of letters he has written to others.
>
> ... I mention unnecessarily, that he is the author of the excellent book *Lands Forlorn* and that he and I have it in common that he has descended the Mackenzie to his field of work, as I to mine, though I only twice and he oftener, and that both of us have wintered in the vicinity of northeastern Great Bear Lake, which is a part of the Rae country.
>
> I hope you all, who receive this letter and its carbons, take my officiousness indulgently.
>
> Vilhjalmur Stefansson.[8]

Not all of those who contacted Douglas about Great Bear and Great Slave Lakes were veterans. In 1955 two young women, Annmarie Krougher and Pamela Russell, from the geography department of McGill University, sought him out for advice about travel on Great Bear Lake. They planned to use a German boat similar to the Inuit kayak, propelled by a double-bladed paddle. Douglas warned them to be cautious, to respect the immense cold lake and to maintain the vigilance necessary for surviving its waters.

The two made a successful trip and came back to Northcote to tell the Douglases about it. Forty-five years earlier Douglas had left his cabin at Hodgson's Point, fully expecting to get back in a year or two. But in all his northern travels he had never again reached it. Now, here were two young women with colour photos of the flowers in bloom on the Barrens; of the cabin built with such care by Lionel; and of the beautiful, powerful lake and the beguiling, beckoning river. Together they poured over the photographs, told stories of the hardships they encountered, and laughed over incidents and ironies of their recent trip and his long-ago one.

Krougher and Russell planned to return, this time with a canoe. Douglas advised them against using an outboard motor on a canoe. He had done it himself, but even with years of experience behind him, he had found it a risky thing. They were expert kayakers but he doubted they had the skill, judgement and strength to tackle Great Bear with a canoe and outboard.

Annmarie Krougher went back to the Barrens the following summer. Pamela Russell did not go, as both her fiance and her father convinced her that once was enough. Instead, another woman, also from McGill, went with her. Their overturned canoe was found near the north-west end of Great Bear Lake. Both women had drowned.

One day in 1955 Douglas chanced to hear a CBC radio broadcast about Edgar Christian and John Hornby by George Whalley, a professor at Queen's University. It stirred old memories and it irked him a little. For each thing the professor said about Hornby, there were a hundred things left unsaid. Moreover, Whalley implied that Hornby was a skilful northern traveller. Hornby was tough, tireless, plucky, agile; and his luck had held for 20 years until the 1927 disaster, but skilful? Never! Douglas wrote to Whalley and, "in a style courteous and firm but a little quizzical," invited him to Northcote. Whalley describes that first visit in his introduction to *The Legend of John Hornby*:

> We were wasting our time he told us, to be interested in Hornby; to think of Hornby
> as a skilful Northern traveller was a mistake. Yet as he talked and the day of our first
> meeting grew on, sitting outdoors at Northcote in the very place where Douglas had
> taken Hornby's photograph thirty years before, Douglas became by indistinguishable
> stages younger – thirty years, forty years; and from the perspective of a past vividly
> recalled and out of a memory uncannily accurate he restored the person of John Hornby
> as he had first known him.[9]

That visit was the first of many over the next seven years. As Douglas's health began to fail in the early 1960s the visits had to be shortened so as not to tire him, but always Whalley went away with more material for his book. During these seven years Whalley gave Douglas a very special gift – the chance to relive his adventures in Coppermine country, on Great Bear and Great Slave Lakes.

When Douglas corresponded with other Northerners he was well aware that the North he had known was almost gone. Theirs was a unique perspective on a land in traumatic transition from the stone age to the age of aviation. In a letter to Stefansson in 1958 he spoke of retaining "... an interest in ship design and propulsion, and also in development in the far North without any wish to smell salt water and even less wish to see the once dearly loved North in its modern guise."[10]

In another letter he wrote: "My life has been one of complete changes from my eighteenth year until the last fifteen years, now I am like a driftwood log thrown up on the beach of my place, far above high water."[11]

By 1960 the simple life of chores at Northcote Farm had become too onerous. Mrs Douglas oversaw the construction of a small house on the edge of Lakefield. They called it Southcote. The farm was sold to their family physician, Dr Hugh Gastle. Douglas himself did not understand that the move was permanent. He considered Southcote "winter quarters" and expected to return to Northcote in the spring. Dr Gastle, who planned to use Northcote as a summer home, told Frances, "If he is well and wants to move out in the spring, let him come."

Early in 1962 Douglas's beloved brother Lionel died in Vancouver. In August of the same year Vilhjalmur Stefansson died of a stroke. Blanchet had died in 1960, Arden and Downes in 1959.

George Whalley brought Douglas a copy of the newly published *The Legend of John Hornby* in the fall of 1962. The old man sat at the kitchen table, leafing through it and studying the pictures. Although he had read the proofs earlier when he was well, he was not able now to read the text. But perhaps his mind went back in time and his feet walked along the Coppermine again.

When spring came, on June 6, 1963, George Douglas died in his sleep.

Douglas's portrait hangs in the National Gallery in Ottawa. Painted by Sir Wyly Grier it pictures George at Northcote, a row of lombardy poplars and a stormy sky behind him. *Master of Northcote*, it is called. Yet the portrait does not suggest a man who stayed home to farm. The artist has caught the look of one who reached for a wider horizon.

The dream he had was an impossible one: to take his cousin's copper empire north without changing or destroying the old North. Like most of those who sought gold, silver, copper, pitchblende and coal on Great Bear and Great Slave Lakes, Douglas never made a rich find for himself or his employers. But he made paths for those who did. He led copper exploration to the shores of the Arctic Sea and around the edges of Great Bear and Great Slave Lakes. He was instrumental in moving the North into the modern age.

In the old North a man travelled on foot or with the power of his own arm on the paddle and he found his own way. In the new North he travelled by airplane with a topographic map in his hand. For Douglas the old North offered the ultimate challenge. He found the new North full of ironies, paradoxes, questions and confusion.

In his photographs and writings, Douglas captured the old North of 1911. Over the next 30 years he focused on the changes that took place there, sometimes with enthusiasm, often with dismay, through the sharp eyes of a veteran and always through the eyes of love.

NOTES

Quotes not footnoted are from George Douglas, *Lands Forlorn*. The Douglas papers are at the Public Archives of Canada.

Chapter 1
1. Caspar Whitney, *On Snow Shoes to the Barren Grounds,* New York, 1896, pp. 1 and 2.

Chapter 3
1. Hornby to Father Ducot, December 28, 1910, quoted in George Whalley, *The Legend of John Hornby,* Macmillan of Canada, Toronto, 1962, p. 55.
2. George Whalley, ''Coppermine Martyrdom,'' *Queen's Quarterly,* Vol. LXVI, No.4, (1960), p. 593.

Chapter 5
1. Thomas Simpson, *Narrative of the Discoveries on the North Coast of America; effected by the Officers of the Hudson's Bay Company During the Years 1836-39,* London, Richard Bentley, 1843.

Chapter 6
1. Father Rouviere to My Lord [Bishop Breynat], Dease River, August 18, 1911. Queen's University Archives.
2. Father Rouviere to Reverend Father [Ducot], Bear Lake, December, 1911. Queen's University Archives.

Chapter 7
1. Father Rouviere to Reverend Father [Ducot], Bear Lake, February 26, 1912. Queen's University Archives.

Chapter 10
1. D'Arcy Arden to George Douglas, July 31, 1918. 2. Denny LaNauze to George Douglas, February 6, 1918.

Chapter 11
Quotations from Denny LaNauze are from his letter to George Douglas February 6, 1918; and from *Report of Inspector LaNauze, 1917* in the *Report* of the North West Mounted Police, Appendix O. Ottawa: 1917.

Chapter 12
1. D'Arcy Arden to George Douglas, December 1, 1918.
2. Arden to Douglas, January 20, 1921.
3. Arden to Douglas, November 20, 1921.
4. John Hornby to George Douglas, May 11, 1926, Queen's University Archives.
5. Guy Blanchet to George Whalley, August 29, 1955, Queen's University Archives.
6. Arden to Douglas, November 10, 1924.
7. Interview with Frances Douglas, 1978.
8. Hornby to Douglas, May 11, 1926.
9. Douglas to Inspector Trundle, RCMP, November 19,1927.
10. Douglas to Hornby (sent to both Fort Smith and Resolution), January 19, 1928.

Chapter 13

1. George Douglas, "Summer Journey along the Southeast Shores of Great Slave Lake", *Canadian Mining and Metallurgical Bulletin,* 1929, p. 3.
2. Douglas to August Sandberg, November 17, 1928, p. 3.
3. Douglas to Sandberg, November 17, 1928, p. 4.
4. George Douglas, "A Summer Journey along the Southeast Shores of Great Slave Lake", p. 3.
5. Douglas to Sandberg, November 17, 1928, p. 5.
6. Douglas, "A Summer Journey along the Southeast Shores of Great Slave Lake", p. 15.
7. George Douglas, "By Canoe and Plane in the Far North" (unpublished paper), pp. 10 and 11.
8. Douglas, "By Canoe and Plane", pp. 12 and 13.

Chapter 14

1. H.S. Wilson to Douglas, November 9, 1928.
2. John Hornby to Margaret Christian, April 11, 1927, Whalley papers, Queen's University Archives.
3. Edgar Christian to Margaret Christian, June 1, 1927, Whalley papers, Queen's University Archives. The original is at Edgar's old school, Dover College, England.
4. J. Hornby, "Notes on the Barren Land Caribou (Rangifer Arcticus)", 1908-19, N.W.T.
5. Arden to Douglas, March 1, 1929.
6. Interview by A.J. Stewart, Yellowknife, 1958, quoted by George Whalley in *The Legend of John Hornby,* Toronto, Macmillan, 1962, p. 127.
7. James Charles Critchell-Bullock to Cartlandt Starnes, August 19, 1928, Queen's University Archives.
8. George Douglas to Vilhjalmur Stefansson, February 9, 1955.

Chapter 15

1. Douglas to Muriel Bigg Wither (his half-sister), March 24, 1932, p. 2. (Andy Cruikshank lost his life in a plane crash en route from Eldorado to Fort Rae in June of 1932.)
2. Douglas to Muriel Bigg Wither, March 24, 1932, p. 2.
3. Douglas, "Flight to Great Bear Lake" (unpublished paper), March 1932, p. 4.
4. Douglas, "Flight to Great Bear Lake", p. 5.
5. Douglas to Muriel Bigg Wither, March 24, 1932, p. 3.
6. Douglas, "Biography", unpublished, prepared for Stefansson, June 11, 1958.
7. Douglas to James Douglas, James Douglas, March 19, 1932, pp. 3-4.
8. Douglas to Muriel Bigg Wither, March 24, 1932, p. 4.
9. Douglas to James Douglas, March 19. 1932, p. 3.
10. Douglas, "Flight to Great Bear Lake", p. 13.
11. Douglas, "Flight to Great Bear Lake", p. 14.
12. Frederick B. Watt, *Great Bear,* a Journey Remembered (Yellowknife: Outcrop, 1980).
13. Douglas, "Flight to Great Bear Lake", p. 14.
14. Douglas to Muriel Bigg Wither, March 24, 1932, p. 5.

15. Douglas to Lionel Douglas, November 6, 1932, p. 3.
16. Douglas to Lionel Douglas, November 6, 1932, p. 2.
17. George Douglas, "Great Bear Lake Revisited", unpublished paper, 1932, pp. 10, 13, 14.
18. Douglas to Denny LaNauze, December 5, 1932, p. 8.
19. Douglas to August Sandberg, December 4, 1933, p. 3.

Chapter 16
1. George Douglas, "Report on Explorations, Athasaska Lake and Great Slave Lake", prepared for Fred Searls, New York, 1935, p. 3.
2. George Douglas, "By Canoe and Plane in the Far North", p. 5.
3. Guy Blanchet to George Whalley, January 17, 1963, Queen's University Archives.

Chapter 17
1. Douglas to Frances Douglas, summer 1938.
2. Douglas to Frances Douglas, summer 1938.
3. Douglas to Frances Douglas, September 18, 1938.
4. Douglas to Frances Douglas, summer 1938.
5. Douglas to Frances Douglas, August 25, 1938. Written aboard the HBC vessel "Dease Lake" en route Yellowknife to Rae.
6. Douglas to Denny LaNauze, August 25, 1938.
7. Douglas to P.G. Downes, January 25, 1951.
8. R.H. Cockburn, "To Great Slave and Great Bear: P.G. Downes's Journal of Travels North from Ile a la Crosse in 1938", Arctic (June 1986), p. 164.
9. Douglas to Frances Douglas, August 25, 1938.
10. George Douglas, "Prospecting Operations of 1938, Great Slave Lake", report for United Verde, p. 5.

Chapter 18
1. Douglas to Downes, Autumn 1938.
2. Frances Douglas "Note on Paul Beaulieu", personal papers.
3. Frances Douglas "Note on Paul Beaulieu".
4. Guy Blanchet, "Great Slave Lake Area, Northwest Territories" (Ottawa: King's Printer, 1926).
5. John Franklin, Captain R.N., F.R.S., *Narrative Of A Journey To The Shores Of The Polar Sea In The Years 1819, 20, 21 and 22,* (London: John Murray, 1823).
6. Warburton Pike, *The Barren Ground of Northern Canada* (New York: E.P. Dutton & Company, 1917), p. 19.
7. P.G. Downes, *Selections From His Writings* (memorial booklet, n.d.), published by The Belmont Hill School, Boston, p. 50.
8. Pike, *The Barren Ground,* pp. 73, 83, 97, 245.
9. Cockburn, "To Great Slave and Great Bear", p. 169.

Chapter 19

1. Prentice G. Downes, Selections, page 6.
2. Cockburn, "To Great Slave and Great Bear", pp. 242, 233, 324, 257, 325, 167.
3. Downes, *Sleeping Island,* pp. 5, 9, 10, 46, 198, 113, 118, 213.
4. Selections, p. 7.
5. Douglas to Downes, July 27, 1952.
6. Douglas to Downes, February. 1951.
7. Douglas to Downes, June 2, 1954.
8. Selections, p. 52.
9. Downes, *Sleeping Island.*

Chapter 20

1. Richard Finnie, note prepared for the author, July 3, 1978.
2. Frances Douglas, note prepared for the author, April 9, 1979.
3. Douglas to Downes, February 8, 1943.
4. Douglas to Downes, March 3, 1951.
5. Douglas to Downes, February 27, 1952.
6. Vilhjalmur Stefansson, *My Life With the Eskimo* (New York: Macmillan, 1913), p. 43.
7. Douglas to Downes, April 28, 1943.
8. Stefansson to Dorothy Middleton, February 9, 1954, Douglas personal papers.
9. Whalley, *The Legend of John Hornby,* p. 3.
10. Douglas to Stefansson, June 11, 1958.
11. Douglas to Mrs. Wakefield, November 9, 1957.

Photo Credits

Plates 70, 94, 112, Mrs. Frances Douglas
Plate 30, Gordon Mallory
Plates 46, 79, Queen's University Archives
All other photos are from the Douglas Collection at the Public Archives of Canada. Researchers may obtain reference numbers by writing to Broadview Press.

Sources

James Mackintosh Bell, *Far Places* (Toronto: Macmillan, 1931).

James Mackintosh Bell, "Report on Great Bear Lake," Geological Survey of Canada (Ottawa, 1901).

Guy Blanchet, *Great Slave Lake Area, Northwest Territories* (Ottawa: King's Printer, 1926).

Guy Blanchet, *Search in the North* (Toronto: Macmillan, 1960).

Agnes Deans Cameron, *The New North* (New York: Appleton, 1910).

Edgar Christian, *Death in the Barren Ground* edited by George Whalley (Ottawa: Oberon, 1980).

R.H. Cockburn, "To Great Slave and Great Bear: P.G. Downes Journal of Travels North from Ile a la Crosse in 1938," in *Arctic*, 1985 and 1986.

Frances Douglas, interviews and biographical notes.

George Douglas, "A Summer Journey Along the Southeast Shores of Great Slave Lake," in the *Canadian Mining and Metallurgical Bulletin* (1929).

George Douglas, "By Canoe and Plane in the Far North, 1928, 1932."

George Douglas, "Flight to Great Bear Lake, March, 1932."

George Douglas, "The First Journey, Great Bear Lake, Summer, 1932."

George Douglas, "Great Bear Lake Revisited, Summer, 1932."

George Douglas, *Lands Forlorn* (New York: Knickerbocker Press, 1914).

George Douglas, "Report on Explorations, Athabaska Lake and Great Slave Lake, 1935."

George Douglas, "Prospecting Operations of 1938, Great Slave Lake."

George Douglas, personal letters to and from D'Arcy Arden, P.G. Downes, Vilhjalmur Stefansson, John Hornby, H.S. Wilson, August Sandber, Guy Blanchet, Frances Douglas and others.

Prentice G. Downes, *Selections from His Writings* (Belmont Hill School).

Prentice G. Downes, *Sleeping Island* (New York, 1943).

Richard Finnie, *Lure of the North* (Philadelphia: David McKay Company, 1940).

John Franklin, *Narrative of a Journey to the Shores of the Polar Sea in the Years 1819, 20, 21 and 22* (London: John Murray, 1823).

David T. Hanbury, *Sport and Travel in the Northland of Canada* (London, 1904).

Bruce Hodgins and Margaret Hobbs, *Nastawgan* (Toronto: Betelgeuse Books, 1985).

J. Hornby, "Notes on the Barren Land Caribou (Rangifer Arcticus)" (N.W.T., 1924).

Warburton Pike, *The Barren Ground of Northern Canada* (London, 1892).

"Report of Inspector LaNauze, 1917," Report of the North West Mounted Police, 1916, Appendix O.

"Rouviere Letters to Bishop Breynat and Father Ducot," Oblates of Mary the Immaculate, Queen's University Archives.

Frank Russell, *Exploration in the Far North* (Iowa, 1898).

Thomas Simpson, *Narrative of the Discoveries on the North Coast of America: effected by the officers of the Hudson's Bay Company during the years 1836-39* (London: Richard Bentley, 1843).

Vilhjalmur Stefansson, *My Life With the Eskimo* (New York: Macmillan, 1936).

Vilhjalmur Stefansson, *The Northward Course of Empire* (New York: Macmillan, 1924).

J.W. Tyrrell, *Report on an Exploratory Survey between Great Slave Lake and Hudson Bay* (Department of the Interior, 1901).

George Whalley, "Coppermine Martyrdom" in *Queen's Quarterly*, Vol. LXVI, No. 4 (1960).

George Whalley, *The Legend of John Hornby* (Toronto: Macmillan, 1962).

George Whalley, "Notes on a Legend," in *Queen's Quarterly*, Vol. LXXVI, No. 4 (Winter, 1970).

Caspar Whitney, *On Snow Shoes to the Barren Grounds* (New York, 1896).

Index

DATE DUE

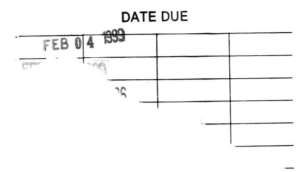

FEB 0 4 1999